STORIES IN THE SAND

SAN FRANCISCO'S SUNSET DISTRICT, 1847–1964

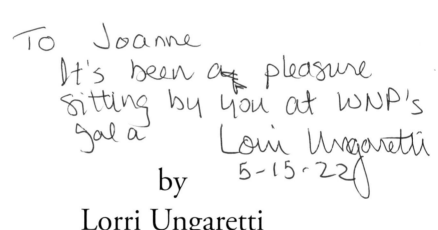

To Joanne
It's been a pleasure
sitting by you at WNP's
gala
Lorri Ungaretti
5-15-22

by

Lorri Ungaretti

Cover design and interior design template by Julie Butts.
Printed by Madison Street Press, Oakland, CA

Front cover photographs used by permission:
Sunset, Judah Street, taken by Dennis Coffen.
Sand dunes, a private collection.
Builders in the sand, Parkside Tavern Collection.
Woman in backyard, San Francisco History Center, San Francisco Public Library.

Library of Congress Control Number: 2011961319
ISBN 978-0-9840016-3-7

Manufactured in the United States of America.

Publisher's Cataloging-in-Publication
(Provided by Quality Books, Inc.)

      Ungaretti, Lorri.
          Stories in the sand : San Francisco's Sunset
      District, 1847-1964 / by Lorri Ungaretti.
            p. cm.
          Includes bibliographical references and index.
          LCCN 2011961319
          ISBN 978-0-9840016-3-7

          1. Sunset District (San Francisco, Calif.)--History.
      2. San Francisco (Calif.)--History.   I. Title.

      F869.S36S85 2012   979.4'61
                                  QBI12-600029

 Balangero Books

          P.O. Box 640076
          San Francisco, CA 94164
          www.balangerobooks.com

STORIES IN THE SAND

SAN FRANCISCO'S SUNSET DISTRICT, 1847–1964

PREFACE

In 2001, I became a City Guide (www.sfcityguides.org), one of many volunteers who lead free walking tours of San Francisco neighborhoods. During the training class, Lisa Buchanan, an experienced guide, asked if anyone was interested in learning how to lead the Inner Sunset tour. Having spent my childhood in the Parkside and having lived in the Inner Sunset in the 1980s, I volunteered. I still lead that tour, and I am still making new discoveries about the neighborhood's history.

Most City Guides take a basic script and then make a tour their own by reading more and providing information about the neighborhood's unique history and features. I assumed that was what I would do, but I found that there were no books on the Sunset and there was almost no historical information available to help me create my own tour. I kept complaining to my mother that there were no books on the Sunset; her reply was "You'll have to write one." After she had said this three or four times, it finally sank in, and I decided to start conducting research on the Sunset.

Thus began a ten-year journey where I met wonderful people who lived or had lived in the Sunset, pored over historical documents, and generally immersed myself in Sunset life and history. This book is the result of those years of research and interviewing. I thank all those people who shared their Sunset experiences with me and all the people in my life who patiently listened to me when I was excited about some new fact or story I had learned.

I would like to express my appreciation to all the people who have helped me over the years. I am indebted to other local historians for their assistance and support, including Jim Ansbro (grandson and advocate of Ray Schiller, the "Mayor of the Parkside"), Richard Brandi, Emiliano Echeverria, Charles Fracchia, John Freeman, Greg Gaar, Katherine Howard of the Golden Gate Park Preservation Alliance, Woody LaBounty, Angus Macfarlane, Tricia O'Brien, Chris Pollock, John Ralston (who first told me about Alice Marble's amazing life), Rand Richards, and Jack Tillmany. Thanks also to my friend and professional copy editor Sherri Schultz, whose eagle eye helped sharpen the text, and Elissa Rabellino, a proofreader who caught many missed details. Merin McDonell and Vicky Walker helped immensely by reviewing the book in its last stages. And, of course, I thank my mother, author Dorothy Bryant, for her encouragement and willingness to read and react to different versions of the book.

I am honored that author Harold Gilliam agreed to write the foreword to this book. A longtime Sunset resident and an amazing writer, Mr. Gilliam was a columnist at the *San Francisco Chronicle* for many years and has written nature books and history books about San Francisco.

The Sunset Education and Action Committee (SPEAK) is the most active and influential Sunset neighborhood advocacy group. SPEAK gave me a grant that helped me to use many of the images I obtained from the San Francisco Public Library.

I also thank all those people and organizations whose photographs and other historical information I was able to use, including Steve Aguado, the Archives of the Archdiocese of San Francisco, the Bancroft Library, Cheryl B. Barr of the Essig Museum of Entomology at the University of California at Berkeley, Robert Bowen, Larry Boysen, Richard Brandi, the California Historical Society, Dennis Coffen, Larry Doyle of Parkside Tavern, Marc Duffett, Emiliano Echeverria, John Freeman, Rosemary French, Ray and Ron Galli, Getty Images, Tom Gray, Gordon Gribble, Ed Hageman, Eileen Hershberg, the History Guild of Daly City/Colma, Jane Hudson, Ann Jennings, the Labor Archives of San Francisco State University, the Lawson-Faulkner family, Richard Lim, the Little Shamrock, Terry Lowry, Charleen Maghzi, Barbara Meli, Dennis Minnick, Cathy Saulovich Morrison, Thomas Murray, Frank and Judy O'Brien, Dennis O'Rorke, Jaci Pappas, Jo Anne Quinn (and her friends who went to St. Cecilia School, including Rita Eastman, Jerry Fleming, John Keenan, Kathy Klingenberg, John Murphy, and Tom O'Toole), Mark Rivero, the San Francisco History Center (San Francisco Public Library), the Ray Schiller family, Grace Guldea Scholz, Shriners Hospital Archives, Jack and Mary Simensen, Alex Spotorno, Alan Thomas, Jack Tillmany, Paul Totah (St. Ignatius College Preparatory), Jeanne Warden, Mark Weinberger, the Western Neighborhoods Project, and the Chas and Ada Williams family.

I am also appreciative of the comfortable chairs and enthusiastic staff of It's a Grind on Polk Street, where I wrote many of these words. And, most of all, I thank the staff, especially Christopher Dougherty, at Madison Street Press in Oakland, California. They all, as usual, did a wonderful and generous job of preparing this book for print and printing it.

Foreword

by Harold Gilliam

Author, Journalist, Environmentalist

Let's face it. The Sunset is not San Francisco's most glamorous district.

It lacks the panache of Telegraph Hill, Union Square, Nob Hill, or the Embarcadero. As a tourist destination it's hardly in the same league with Fisherman's Wharf, North Beach, Russian Hill, Chinatown, or even the newly transformed South of Market.

Yet the Sunset is a solid, substantial family neighborhood with its own history, traditions, institutions, and landmarks. Before moving here, I had lived in Pacific Heights, Telegraph Hill, and the Haight-Ashbury, and like many people I chose the Sunset to settle down and raise a family.

After 50 years in the Sunset, I thought I knew everything there was to know about it. I was wrong. Lorri Ungaretti, who grew up here, has done a years-long job of intensive research, pored over innumerable documents, interviewed dozens of old-time residents, and written what must be the Sunset's definitive history.

You will learn here, for example, about how the area was originally thought to be a desert of uninhabitable sand dunes and about the original settlers who nevertheless braved wind, fog, and sandstorms to "homestead" in the dunes. It was then federal land that was considered to be "out west" from San Francisco. The effort of the city to claim these "Outside Lands" was a decades-long legal battle with the federal government before the boundaries of the city were finally extended to the ocean.

It was Mike de Young, publisher of the *San Francisco Chronicle*, who envisioned the possibilities of the Sunset and promoted the idea of a world's fair in the new Golden Gate Park, at the Sunset's northern boundary. The fair drew millions of people in 1894 and encouraged commercial and residential building in the adjacent district. It was not until the 1930s and 1940s that the subdivisions were extended westward to Ocean Beach by such builders as Henry Doelger, who specialized in standard-design homes affordable to young families. Doelger showed his high opinion of the Sunset by building a home there for his own family.

A few sand dunes remained, however, through the 1950s, and Ungaretti remembers trudging through one of them as a child living across the street from Lincoln High School. Long-time residents told her that in the early days the roar of the lions at the San Francisco Zoo could be heard at night across the district. Some of them remembered how the kids used to play in the "mountains of sand" and frequented swimming holes at places where creeks from inland were dammed by the highest dunes en route to the ocean.

Like most histories, this one is not all sweetness and light. Ungaretti describes how restrictions on who could rent or buy in the neighborhood were written into original house deeds and discusses a statewide battle over whether racial minorities could legally be excluded from residential areas such as the Sunset. The practice involved a statewide election and ultimately became a test case in the courts.

Ungaretti profiles some of the people who lived in the Sunset years ago. For example, the award-winning tennis player Alice Marble grew up in the Inner Sunset and had an adventurous life. We also learn about the neighborhood's registered landmarks and other fascinating buildings, including St. Anne of the Sunset, the large church that can be seen for miles and features a frieze conceived and created by a Bay Area Dominican nun.

If you're a resident of the Sunset, I would recommend an observation by writer Wendell Berry: "You don't know who you are, until you know where you are." Read this book and find out who and where you are.

—Harold Gilliam, 2012

Chapter 1

The Great Sand Bank

Before the twentieth century, more than half of San Francisco was covered in sand dunes. Some dunes were more than 100 feet deep, some more than 60 feet high. Today you can dig down a few feet in many areas of the city and find sand.

Most of San Francisco's sand was concentrated in the north and west edges of the peninsula. The most obvious and undisturbed area of sand until the mid-twentieth century lay in the Sunset District, part of what was known as the Outside Lands. In fact, the only area in the Sunset that is not composed of sand is the hilly eastern section known as Golden Gate Heights. Here the hills are composed of chert, a sedimentary bedrock, covered in sand.

Where did all this sand come from? Some of it came from the cliffs south of San Francisco, constantly moved northward to San Francisco's Ocean Beach by ocean currents. However, most of the sand traveled more than 100 miles from the mountains of the Sierra Nevada thousands of years ago. During the last ice age, perhaps 20,000 years ago, "the granitic rocks of the Sierra Nevada were ground down by glaciers, and the resulting sediment was carried off by great rivers … the small sand grains traveled westward, carried by tributaries to the Sacramento and San Joaquin Rivers, then across the Central Valley, through the Carquinez Strait, and out to the ocean."[1]

The Sunset District looking west, long before it developed into today's neighborhood.

Twelve thousand years ago, the San Francisco shoreline was more than 30 miles west of where it is now. (Today's Farallon Islands were on dry land.) Thousands of years ago, the sand was deposited on that dry land west of the San Francisco peninsula, and later it was picked up by the winds and blown across the city.

A recent mapping of the Pacific Ocean floor shows that sand dunes exist not only on land but also below the water (where they are called sand waves) just west of the edge of San Francisco.[2] Over time, ocean currents moved the sand inland, and strong winds blew the sand eastward and through much of San Francisco. Some of the city's hills stopped the sand's migration, which explains why so much of the sand remained in the west.

THE TREES OF SAN FRANCISCO

Imagine San Francisco with no tall trees. No Golden Gate Park foliage. No tree-covered hills like Mount Sutro and Mount Davidson. That was how San Francisco looked in 1848 when the Gold Rush attracted thousands of people to California—and to San Francisco. A few short trees were scattered here and there, but the landscape comprised mostly sand dunes and low-growing plants. William H. Green (sometimes spelled Greene) started planting trees in the 1870s. Other early residents, most notably Adolph Sutro, later changed the landscape by planting thousands of trees.

This 1886 view of the Inner Sunset shows no tall trees on Mount Sutro (left, which Sutro called Mount Parnassus) and Mount Davidson (center rear, then called Blue Mountain). The photograph shows the home (and hog farm) of Cornelius Reynolds, a watchman for the Market Street Railway, near 14th Avenue.

THE FOG BELT

This 1865 view from the Cliff House shows the pattern of western sand dunes.

Another deterrent to the early development of the Sunset was the heavy fog. While other San Francisco neighborhoods experience at least partially sunny days, the Sunset District often sits under a thick, cold fog, especially during the summer months.

Residents today frequently complain about summer fog, but in the late 1800s and early 1900s the fog was not just unappealing; it could be deadly. An 1897 newspaper reported that a woman had died when she lost her way in the dunes after the fog blew in. According to the article, the woman had set out from the Alms House (now Laguna Honda Hospital), and after she reached the Sunset, "footprints in the sand showed that she had wandered round and round in a circle until overcome by exhaustion and cold."[3] Without the streets, signs, and lights that crowd the area now, someone walking through the sand dunes when the fog blew in would find it hard to tell which way was west (the beach), north (Golden Gate Park), or east—back to the Almshouse.

DISPUTED OWNERSHIP

In the middle 1800s, San Franciscans pretty much ignored the Outside Lands, not only because of the area's inaccessibility but also because the area did not belong to the City of San Francisco. The Outside Lands were originally controlled by Spain and then by Mexico. In 1848, the Treaty of Guadalupe Hidalgo gave California to the United States, and ownership of the Outside Lands became disputed. Did the federal government or the City of San Francisco own the land?

Residential growth in the Outside Lands was slow. A few houses were scattered along the beach, which people could access from the north and south. A few more houses dotted the area later known as the Inner Sunset—miles to the east, closer to downtown. Most people considered the foggy sand dunes uninhabitable.

In 1852, as San Francisco was rapidly growing, city leaders began a struggle to clarify the ownership of the San Francisco peninsula. The city would fight the federal government in the courts for almost fifteen years before the case was settled.

"There was a time, now many years ago, when San Francisco halted far east of Van Ness Avenue, and with the exception of the Presidio and the settlement around the old Mission Dolores, there was nothing to be seen but miles of sand dunes, and the afternoon winds lifted their shifting surface and swept it through the streets of the city."

—

Gertrude Atherton,
My San Francisco: A Wayward Biography, p. 26

"At the distance of from 2 to 5 miles from the city, over the sand hills, in the direction of the Pacific coast, there are some 20 or 30 little wooden shanties, scattered at intervals of half a mile or a mile apart. Situated in the little gulches between the hills, or concealed from view by the shrubbery, few know of their existence except the hunters who stroll over the hills in quest of game. A man might pass within a few hundred yards of them every day, and never see them, nor dream of their existence. These desolate huts have become the dens and abiding places of thieves and outcasts. An escaped convict, or a suspected felon, may remain secluded and secure for weeks and months amongst them. ... their isolated position enables them to make frequent secret visits to the city, for the purposes of robbery or to dispose of their ill-gotten gain."

—

"Haunts of Robbers,"
Daily Alta California,
January 15, 1858

Once a common sight in San Francisco's Sunset District, the Xerces Blue butterfly became extinct in the 1940s due to the development of the neighborhood.

"Why tell the story of a vanished butterfly? Because it illustrates what happens when an organism is adapted to a naturally limited habitat and that habitat becomes valuable for human uses; if no one is paying attention and speaking up for the little folks, the organism loses. Once it is gone, its story goes, robbing us of the knowledge to be gained from its life."

—

Susan J. Tweit,
*Seasons on the Pacific Coast:
A Naturalist's Notebook,* pp. 81–82

CONSEQUENCES OF RAPID DEVELOPMENT

Developers began to build on the sand in the twentieth century, and by 1950 most of the Sunset was covered with streets, houses, schools, and other buildings. This rapid development destroyed some native plants, insects, and animals that had flourished in the dunes. For example, the Xerces Blue is believed to be the first butterfly to become extinct because of human development. Once common in western San Francisco, "by the 1930s, the butterfly was restricted to vacant lots."[4] The Xerces Blue was last seen in the Presidio in 1941. Another butterfly, the Green Hairstreak, was once common in San Francisco but now is found only in Golden Gate Heights (the hills just east of the Sunset District street grid) and in the Presidio. As houses covered the sand dunes, native plants, such as coast buckwheat and the seaside daisy, became rare or disappeared, as did the area's insects and birds that had to find other habitats or become extinct.

Some of the plants that still exist and once flourished in the Sunset District are endangered today, including the Franciscan wallflower (also called the San Francisco wallflower) and the dune tansy.

Most of the land south of Golden Gate Park remained undeveloped well into the twentieth century, but Adolph Sutro and others covered the nearby hills and gullies with nonnative trees and plants during the late 1800s. Mount Sutro and Mount Davidson, both easily visible from the Inner Sunset, host dense forests that "all but destroyed the biologically rich North Coastal Scrub and wildflower communities that had evolved for thousands of years"[5] on these hills.

This 1930s photo looks east from the sand lot that would become Lincoln High School. Although frequently referred to simply as scrub brush, the plant life in the dunes was rich and varied. This photo shows the once-prevalent dune tansy (now rare), as well as the Chamisso bush lupine, monkey flower, and coyote bush.[6]

Looking southwest in 1943 from what would become 33rd Avenue near Pacheco Street. Some building has begun in the background, but most of the area is still sand dunes. Many people used the wide-open land to dump garbage, some of which is visible in the foreground.

Low trees and bushes grew in the Sunset sand. This photograph was taken at what is now 32nd Avenue and Santiago Street.

Notes

1. Doris Sloan, *Geology of the San Francisco Bay Region*, pp. 119–23.

2. Glen Martin, "City's Beautiful but Hidden Sand Dunes," *San Francisco Chronicle*, July 20, 2006, p. A-1.

3. "A Veritable Desert in the City of San Francisco," *San Francisco Call*, May 23, 1897, p. 27.

4. http://www.kuhmann.com/Butterfly/Glaucopsyche%20lygdamus%20xerces.htm

5. Greg Gaar, "The Sunset: From Windy Wasteland to Bustling Boomtown," *Sunset Beacon*, January 1992, p. 14.

6. Special thanks to Greg Gaar for identifying the plant life in this photograph and for sharing his extensive knowledge of plants native to San Francisco.

CHAPTER 2

THE OUTSIDE LANDS
BECOME PART OF SAN FRANCISCO

With the discovery of gold in California, the population of San Francisco grew from about 800 in 1848 to more than 20,000 in 1850 and to 50,000 by 1860. All but a few residents lived in the eastern part of the city.

In 1850, the California legislature approved San Francisco's charter, which made Larkin and 9th Streets the city's western boundary. A year later, a city reincorporation moved the western boundary to Devisadero (now Divisadero) Street (hence the neighborhood named the Western Addition). All the land outside these city limits, called the Outside Lands, included not only the areas west of Twin Peaks but also parts of the Mission, Western Addition, Haight-Ashbury, and other neighborhoods.*

The areas now known as the Richmond District, Golden Gate Park, and the Sunset District were sometimes described as a "cold desert," an uninhabitable sand waste. Fog often blew in over the dunes and gusty winds scattered the sand. An 1850s map of San Francisco labeled the western part of the city the "Great Sand Bank."

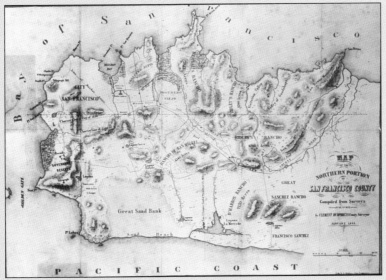

This map, drawn in 1853, described the Outside Lands as the "Great Sand Bank."

* At one time, the Outside Lands referred to all land adjacent to but outside the San Francisco city limits. Now just the Richmond District, Golden Gate Park, and the Sunset District are considered the Outside Lands.

In 1851, Congress established the U.S. Land Commission to "settle private land claims in the state of California." The following year, on July 2, San Francisco filed a Petition for Pueblo Grant, arguing that the government of Mexico in 1833 had granted San Francisco pueblo status. If San Francisco were truly a pueblo under old Mexican law, it was entitled to "four square leagues of land" (about 28 square miles), which would include the Outside Lands, at that time claimed by the federal government.

For years, local alcaldes (predecessors to mayors) had been selling land grants under the assumption that the city owned the land. If San Francisco did not succeed in its effort to be recognized as a pueblo, these land grants would be nullified. According to Stephen Field, later a California and then U.S. Supreme Court justice, "The whole community was in fact divided between those who asserted the existence of a pueblo having a right to the lands mentioned, and the power of alcaldes to make grants of them; and those who insisted that the land belonged to the United States."[1]

In December 1854, the U.S. Land Commission confirmed San Francisco's claim to pueblo lands but granted only three square leagues instead of the requested four. In August 1855, the U.S. government appealed the ruling to the U.S. District Court on the grounds that the city did not own additional land; the city appealed, insisting that it did own title to more land.

The case wandered through the courts for almost fifteen years. Some court decisions favored the city's claim but did not provide for the full acreage the city wanted. Other decisions denied that San Francisco was a pueblo and concluded that the city should not own or control additional land. When the U.S. government lost a ruling, it appealed; when the City of San Francisco lost a ruling, it appealed.

In March 1858 the California Supreme Court, in *Hart v. Burnett,* held that San Francisco was "a fully organized pueblo" and entitled to four square leagues. This was a step toward granting the contested land to San Francisco. Once again, though, the U.S. government appealed, this time to the U.S. Circuit Court, which, in October 1864, ruled in favor of the City of San Francisco. Judge Stephen Field, who wrote the opinion, later wrote:

> I held that a pueblo of some kind existed at the site of the present city of San Francisco upon the cession of the country; that as such it was entitled to the possession of certain lands to the extent of four square leagues ... I accordingly decided that the city was entitled to have her claim confirmed to four square leagues of land, subject to certain reservations ... But I also added that the lands to which she was entitled ... [were] to be held in trust for the benefit of the whole community.[2]

In October 1865, Justice Field received a package that contained an explosive ("a torpedo"). He detected the danger and was not hurt. He later wrote, "On the inside of the lid was pasted a slip from a San Francisco paper, dated October 31st, 1864, stating that on the day previous I had decided the case of the City against the United States, involving its claims to four square leagues of land, and giving the opening lines of my opinion." Field added that the sender may have been seeking "a late vengeance for the decision of the Pueblo case" or might have been "some guilty person who ... used the reference to the Pueblo case to divert suspicion from himself." [3]

The United States filed an appeal to the U.S. Supreme Court on May 18, 1865. While the case was in the Supreme Court docket, California Senator John Conness introduced a bill ordering that the federal government's claim to the pueblo lands be "relinquished and granted to the city of San Francisco." This bill passed on March 8, 1866, ending the court battle but adding a restriction on San Francisco's use of the land: the city could set aside lands for public uses, but the remaining land "shall be disposed of and conveyed by said city to parties in the bona fide actual possession thereof, by themselves or tenants … in such quantities and upon such terms and conditions as the Legislature of the State of California may prescribe."[4]

WHAT TO DO WITH THE OUTSIDE LANDS

Squatters, hopeful residents, speculators, and investors all had interest in and claimed rights to parts of the Outside Lands. Now that the land was owned by San Francisco, questions remained about how it would be distributed. Whatever plan the city devised had to be approved by the state legislature.

On December 2, 1867, the San Francisco Board of Supervisors appointed its first Committee on Outside Lands. The list of committee members over time reads like a "Who's Who" of San Francisco street names: Charles Stanyan, A. J. Shrader, R. Beverly Cole, Monroe Ashbury, R. P. Clement, and Charles Clayton.

The first committee recommended assessing the land, dividing it into blocks, and setting some aside for public use. Some of the committee's recommendations became part of Order No. 800, which the board of supervisors passed in January 1868 and the California State Legislature later confirmed.

Under Order No. 800, the city hired George C. Potter and William P. Humphreys to survey the Outside Lands and create a map showing streets, lots, and areas set aside for public use. In what became the Sunset District, two areas were set aside for parks (later McCoppin Square and Parkside Square), fifteen for "fire engine lots," and more than forty for schools. This map, produced in 1868, was on display for public inspection for thirty days so that people who believed they owned property in the Outside Lands could make their claims.

San Francisco newspapers printed announcements about the Outside Lands Map, which was available for public review. This announcement read: "All persons interested in OUTSIDE LANDS are hereby notified to have their Claims immediately delineated on the Map of Outside Lands, in accordance with the provisions of Order No. 800, as all blank spaces on said Map will be considered as entirely Free of any and all Claims and will be so treated." The notice was signed by C. H. Stanyan, chairman of the Committee on Outside Lands.

NOTICE TO HOLDERS OF OUTSIDE LANDS.

ALL PERSONS INTERESTED IN OUTSIDE LANDS are hereby notified to have their Claims immediately delineated on the Map of Outside Lands, in accordance with the provisions of Order No. 800, as all blank spaces on said Map will be considered as entirely free of any and all Claims, and will be so treated.

C. H. STANYAN,
Chairman of Committee of the Board of Supervisors on Outside Lands.

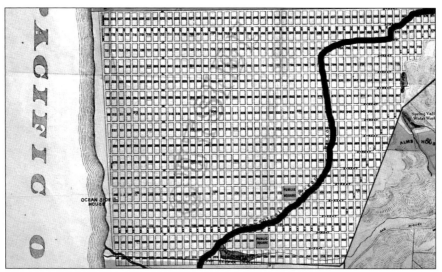

This 1875 map of the Sunset District shows the now-familiar grid pattern of blocks and streets, but none of these streets had yet been built. The only road that ran through the Sunset was the Central Ocean Road (see dark line), which started at what is now the Golden Gate Park panhandle, zigzagged through the Sunset, and ended at Ocean Road on the south. The southern part of the road ended just south of Pine Lake in what is now Sigmund Stern Grove/Pine Lake Park. (See Pine Lake in the bottom center of the map.)

THE VAN NESS ORDINANCE AND THE MCCOPPIN PLAN

In 1851, San Francisco extended its western border from Larkin and 9th Streets to Divisadero Street. In 1855, James P. Van Ness, San Francisco alderman and later mayor (Van Ness Avenue is named after him), introduced what became known as the Van Ness Ordinance, which set aside the additional land for public uses but granted the remaining property to people who could prove they had actual possession of the land on or before January 1, 1855. Passed by the San Francisco Board of Supervisors in June 1855, the Van Ness Ordinance was ratified by the California State Legislature in 1858 and by Congress in 1864.

In 1866, when the Outside Lands became part of the City of San Francisco, many believed that the Van Ness Ordinance would apply so that residents and others claiming to own property in the Outside Lands would simply be allowed to keep their land. Others believed that no one should be allowed to own more than 50 acres, regardless of how much land they had "owned" earlier. Eventually a new plan was devised, one that would bring money into city coffers.

The McCoppin Plan, proposed by San Francisco Supervisor Frank McCoppin (elected mayor in 1867), allowed Outside Lands property claimants to keep their land if

- they could "verify by oath or affirmation" that they were in possession of the land as of March 8, 1866;

- they gave 10 percent of their land to the city for public parks; and

- they paid a tax of 10 percent of the value of the land.

The board of supervisors approved the Mc-Coppin Plan in 1869 and the California State Legislature ratified it in 1870. After setting aside lands for schools, hospitals, fire stations, and parks, the city benefited from the taxes paid by Outside Lands residents. At the same time, the additional land obtained by the city made it possible to build a large park in the Outside Lands.

> *"I lived at the time on my farm [now Sigmund Stern Grove], some seven or eight miles from the City, and I would generally ride in in the morning and return to my farm in the evening."*
>
> —
>
> Alfred Green, *Life and Adventures of a 47-er of California,* p. 43

The area was changing, as noted by a newspaper reporter in 1897:

A visit to this desert, for such it really is, will well repay the effort required. To get into the heart of it is no child's play and a person not a good walker and climber must give up all idea of ever doing so. ... It is hard walking. ... Over one hill and down another. Sights and sounds of civilization gradually disappear until at last the traveler is alone. ... Standing on some of the highest sandhills it is possible to look over a large area, and it is seldom that a human footprint can be seen. ...

In many parts of the desert there are acres and acres without the least sign of vegetation. .... The places where there is any vegetation to speak of are in hollows between the sandhills ... There is no more desolate spot on earth than the heart of this region. ... The silence is almost absolute, except for the muffled beating of the surf that comes monotonously over the dreary dunes. ... In one sense the desert is at present a useless waste, but it is not destined to remain so very long. The march of improvement is going that way and soon it will be cut up into building lots. This knowledge may cause the nature lover, as he turns his back upon the desert, a feeling of regret.[5]

NOTES

1. Stephen J. Field, *California Alcalde,* p. 110.
2. Ibid., p. 114.
3. Ibid., p. 171.
4. John W. Dwinelle, *Colonial History [of the] City of San Francisco,* p. 313.
5. "A Veritable Desert in the City of San Francisco," *San Francisco Call,* May 23, 1897, p. 27.

Some of the land set aside in the late 1860s for the new Golden Gate Park.

"Today's tapestry of buildings, meadows, and gardens is far from the original state of the northwest tip of the San Francisco peninsula, for which a more appropriate name would have been 'Sand Francisco.'... the sparsely populated and virtually treeless landscape of windswept, rolling dunes gave no hint of the potential for greenery."

—

Christopher Pollock, *San Francisco's Golden Gate Park*, p. 19

CHAPTER 3

CREATING GOLDEN GATE PARK

It is impossible today to imagine San Francisco without Golden Gate Park. Though technically not part of the Sunset District, it runs along the entire northern border of the Sunset (Lincoln Way) and, since its creation, has provided a resource for recreation and green space for thousands of Sunset residents. Golden Gate Park counters the misconception that the Sunset District is "wall-to-wall concrete."

When the courts and legislature granted the Outside Lands to San Francisco in 1866, the board of supervisors sent a letter to Frederick Law Olmsted, designer of Central Park in New York City and Mountain View Cemetery in Oakland, "to obtain his views and recommendations as to extent of grounds required, and suitable location for a Park." Olmsted visited San Francisco and wrote,

> There is not a full-grown tree of beautiful proportions near San Francisco, nor have I seen any young trees that promised fairly, except perhaps, of certain compact, clumpy forms of evergreens, wholly wanting in grace and cheerfulness. It would not be wise nor safe to undertake to form a park upon any plan which assumed as a certainty that trees which would delight the eye can be made to grow near San Francisco."[1]

In one respect, Olmsted was right: in the 1860s there were no tall trees in San Francisco. While we currently see a variety of eucalyptus, pine, cypress, redwood, and other imposing trees on Mount Sutro and Mount Davidson, in Golden Gate Park and Sigmund Stern Grove (and throughout San Francisco), these trees are not native to the city. Anyone designing and building a large park in the Outside Lands needed the imagination to believe that plants and trees could grow in the sand dunes.

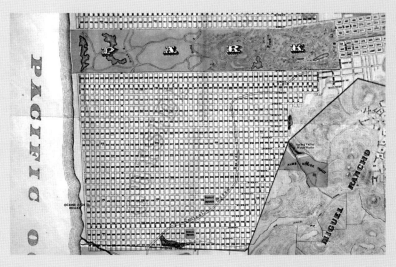

This 1875 Langley map shows Golden Gate Park, with the Sunset District on the south and the Pacific Ocean on the west.

Olmsted recommended a large park in another area of San Francisco, where the weather was better and sand dunes were shallower, but in its report dated January 6, 1867, the Committee on Outside Lands recommended that part of the Outside Lands be converted into a large city park. The California State Legislature agreed; in 1870, it set the boundaries for "the Golden Gate Park," using that name for the first time and ratifying a plan to build the park on 1,017 acres of the Outside Lands.

William Hammond Hall.

After Olmsted declined to build a park in the Outside Lands, the city turned to engineer William Hammond Hall, who was confident that he could "tame" the sand dunes and transform them into a verdant park.

The *Bulletin* newspaper reported in January 1866 that sandy property in Ireland and France was similar to San Francisco's Outside Lands (a "waste of lands covered with shifting sands") and that *Pinus maritima,* a type of pine, had helped prepare Irish and French land for planting. "At the present time," the reporter wrote, "when it is expected that the outside lands of the city are about to be apportioned among our citizens in small homesteads, information like the above becomes very interesting. ... If a few of our citizens would join together to procure the seeds of the French variety ... in one short year from now plants of this valuable tree may be already peeping above the surface upon hundreds of homesteads between the Western Addition and the Pacific Ocean."[2]

A later article in a competing newspaper described how these pine seeds were tested in Golden Gate Park, noting that they "rendered good service in preventing [sand] drift. ... With evidence of what has been done abroad and the successful experiment at our own doors it is evident that every foot of sand waste from the ocean beach inland can be reclaimed and made beautiful with forests and valuable timber. There is hope for a successful Park, even if made out of these, at present, sandy, desolate wastes."[3]

Grading the land for Golden Gate Park in the 1870s.

William Hammond Hall described some of what he saw on the uncultivated land set aside for the park: "On the eastern part of the central hill, there was a ramshackle, tumble-down little house, where an old, heavily-whiskered hermit-like man lived, with several dogs for companions. Chickens and ducks, which he raised there, and large frogs which he caught in the ponds out towards the beach and sold to French restaurants, yielded him a livelihood. ... A few jack rabbits, cottontails and quail found refuge on the scrub-covered hills."[4]

Work on the park began in 1871, starting with the eastern Panhandle, then called "the Avenue." Gardeners first planted lupine seeds to stop the dunes from drifting, but the lupine grew so slowly that the sand often buried it. A popular story is that some barley fell from a horse bag onto the sand, sprouted quickly, and showed gardeners that they could use a mixture of barley and lupine seed to settle the dunes. The sprouted barley allowed water-soaked lupine to gain a stronghold in the sand. Once the lupine had grown, it settled some of the sand and made planting possible. This story may be true or may be folklore. The French pine seed (see facing page) was used, at least initially. Perhaps gardeners also used the barley and lupine method.

Opposition to a park in the Outside Lands took many forms. City residents complained that it was too far from the center of the city. Public transportation to the Outside Lands was minimal or nonexistent. Other people complained about the weather, noting that the climate in the Mission and other districts was more conducive to outdoor activities.

Dr. Isaac Rowell, a member of the board of supervisors, called "this talk about a 3,000 acre park"* absurd. He said, "God Almighty never intended there should be parks here, and we have no use for them."

"Today, it is difficult to visualize the immensity of the areas set aside for the park and the problems in building it up from raw ground. ... The entire area was windswept nearly all the time. When a stiff breeze sprang up, it was difficult to get a horse to face west because of the blowing sand. Aside from a few homesteaders, visitors to the area were few—except for young boys who liked to explore their 'Sahara Desert.' Other boys and men visited the natural lakes in the sand dunes to shoot ducks and gather wild rice and frog legs to be sold to the French restaurants around the city."

—

Raymond Clary,
*The Making of Golden Gate Park,
The Early Years: 1865–1906*, p. 12

"The Oak Woodlands in Golden Gate Park are the remnants of the only 'forested' area originally within the 49 square miles of San Francisco. These coastal live oaks grow in sheltered ravine areas and, remarkably, were left intact when Golden Gate Park was created by removing all the native dune plant communities and planting non-native grasses and ornamental plants."

—

San Francisco Recreation and
Park Department,
http://sfnaturalareas.org/sites/4

* The park was originally 1,013 acres and later enlarged to 1,017 acres, but it was never the 3,000 acres Rowell described.

"[If] someone had the temerity to suggest at that time that within fifteen years Golden Gate Park would become famous, he or she would have been rushed off to an insane asylum."

—

Raymond Clary,
The Making of Golden Gate Park, The Early Years: 1865–1906, p. 13

"Market and Fifth streets were once considered out in the wilderness. Then they were sand dunes, and our city then had croakers who warned enterprising buyers against going 'too far out.' ... the extreme Western Addition was a place to be avoided on windy days, for the sand blew with every gust and forming banks, drifted like snow ... The planting of grass, trees and shrubs, erection of fences and houses, leveling and grading of streets, soon changed the aspect and condition of the region, however. So it will be with Southside [an early name for the Sunset District] some day."

—

San Francisco Chronicle,
May 24, 1891, p. 18

For a while, real estate interests (who wanted to develop the land) opposed the building of Golden Gate Park, calling it the "Great Sand Park." However, as the park grew, it gathered more public support. By the late 1870s, people were coming from all over the city to visit the popular sprawling park. An 1875 newspaper article praised the growing park: "Thousands of little plants ... may be seen now by the close observer flourishing in what was, less than two years ago, a barren, drifting sand desert. ... The reclamation of the sand dunes is a most important feature in the construction of the park." The article noted that 600 people visited Golden Gate Park every weekday and 1,000 to 1,200 on Sundays.[5] Many of these visitors enjoyed the Park Panorama ("Sweeny's Observatory"), built on Strawberry Hill in 1891. From this spot, viewers could see a 360-degree view of the surrounding areas. The observatory was created with funding from Thomas Sweeny, a Sunset resident who lived at 7th Avenue and J (now Judah) Street. The Park Panorama was destroyed by the 1906 earthquake.

Scottish immigrant John McLaren started working as assistant superintendent of Golden Gate Park in 1887 and was appointed superintendent in 1890. He served for 53 years, defining the park's purpose as a sylvan retreat from city life. He retired shortly before his death in 1943. San Francisco's 312-acre McLaren Park was named in his honor.

Sweeny's Observatory atop Strawberry Hill gave visitors an unobstructed, 360-degree view.

Early Golden Gate Park visitors.

THE 1894 MIDWINTER FAIR

In 1894 San Francisco hosted the California Midwinter International Exposition (also called the Midwinter Fair) in Golden Gate Park. The country was suffering from an economic depression, and a fair in San Francisco provided jobs and attracted people from around the country. It also drew many San Franciscans to the rarely visited west side of the city.

The fair's groundbreaking ceremony was held on August 24, 1893, in the area now known as the Music Concourse. One of the main entrances was at 9th Avenue and H Street (now Lincoln Way). Featuring many exhibits from the 1893 Columbian Exposition in Chicago, the fair officially opened on January 27, 1894 and ran until July 4, drawing more than two million attendees.

The groundbreaking in 1893 for the California Midwinter International Exposition brought thousands of people to Golden Gate Park.

The 1894 Midwinter Fair was promoted heavily by M. H. de Young, owner of the *San Francisco Chronicle* newspaper and of land south of the park. The fair helped raise awareness of the area, and after the fair closed, de Young and other landowners were able to attract land and home buyers.

"When I was little, they were using the windmills to pump water into Golden Gate Park. The park supervisor, John McLaren, was alive when I was young. He built the park and had the politicians doing what he wanted. There used to be bears and cages of other animals in the park. Later, some of them were taken to the zoo, but I remember seeing these animals. It was really very sad because no one ever visited them. You would all of a sudden come across these bears or whatever was there. It must have been pretty lonesome."

—

Valerie Meehan (born 1924)

One exhibit built for the Midwinter Exposition that still thrives today is the Japanese Tea Garden. George Turner Marsh, a Richmond District resident and collector of Japanese art, came up with the idea of the fair's Japanese Village. Makito Hagiwara transformed the exhibit into the Japanese Tea Garden and ran it for many years. (For more information about Hagiwara and the tea garden, see pages 100–101.)

Over the years, Golden Gate Park has become an integral part of San Francisco and a "backyard" for residents of the Richmond and Sunset Districts. Called "the jewel of the city," the park draws visitors from around the world. Voters almost always pass bond issues to support its maintenance and improvement. In addition to the abundance of trees and meadows found in many parks, visitors enjoy a botanical garden, an AIDS Memorial Grove, a conservatory of flowers, museums, walking and bicycle paths, and more. Entire books have been written about the history, development, and features of Golden Gate Park.[6]

The park has often been eyed for various development projects. To protect the bucolic character of the park, the City of San Francisco adopted the Golden Gate Park Master Plan in 1998, after an extensive ten-year public process.

The Japanese Village was one of the exhibits at the 1894 Midwinter Fair.

THE SUNSET NAME

Early developers used different names to describe the area south of Golden Gate Park. Names included South of the Park, Strawberry Heights, Sunset Heights, Parkside, Southside, the Byfield Tract, and Sunset Valley. The origin of the name Sunset District is not known. Developers Aurelius Buckingham and Sol Getz claimed at various times to have named the district, but some historians dispute their claims.[7]

Two other origins of the Sunset name seem plausible. One theory focuses on the Midwinter Exposition of 1894. As the fairgrounds were being built, newspapers began referring to the fair as "the exposition," "Palm City," and "the grounds." In October 1893, the *San Francisco Examiner* called it "The Sunset City," a name that seemed to stick. By the time the fair ended, the Sunset name may have become synonymous with the area south of the park.

Another theory focuses on a neighborhood community group. In the 1890s landowners and developers used a variety of names to refer to what is now called the Inner Sunset. These names were originally connected to the landowners: for example, the Buckingham Block, the Byfield Tract, the Sweeny Tract, the Richardson Tract, and the Berton Tract. As developers began to market this area, other names appeared: Sunset Heights and Sunset Valley, as well as South Side and Parkside, the last two referring to Golden Gate Park. South Side was the most popular, and a landowners' advocacy group, the South Side Improvement Club (also called South of the Park Improvement Association), was formed in 1887.

In the summer of 1895, a group of local residents was campaigning for streetcar service and other improvements to the area. They gathered at a meeting hall at 9th Avenue and H Street and decided that they wanted to distinguish their group, which was composed of people who lived in the neighborhood,[8] from the existing South Side Improvement Club, which was primarily composed of absentee land owners and speculators. "One member, Gus Fox, suggested they name themselves the Sunset District Improvement Club in honor of a magnificent sunset the group's members had just watched." In those days, there were no trees, no overhead electrical wires, and few buildings in the area. The land sloped naturally toward the ocean on the west. On a clear or partly cloudy day, a sunset could be stunning. The group that met on that summer evening decided to call itself the Sunset District Improvement Club, and the Sunset name first appeared in print in September 1895. The South Side and Parkside names were taken over by other neighborhoods, the first by a group south of Market Street, and the second by a group in the Sunset just north of what is now Sigmund Stern Grove.

Originally, the Sunset District comprised what is today's Inner Sunset: "from First avenue [Arguello] west to Sixteenth avenue, and from H Street [Lincoln] south to O [Ortega] street. ... Seventh avenue ... passes through the heart of the Sunset District."[9] As dunes were leveled and covered with housing, and streets cut through, the district grew to include more land.

A series of 1893 lithographs illustrated the Midwinter Fair. The lower right side of this image shows Golden Gate Park. The upper left-hand side shows the Sunset District, at that time just sand dunes south of the park.

NOTES

1. *San Francisco Municipal Reports, 1865–66*, p. 397.

2. "How to Reclaim the Sand-hills on the City's Outside Lands," *The Bulletin*, January 6, 1866, p. 2.

3. "A Practical Demonstration," *Daily Alta California*, May 23, 1868, p. 1.

4. William Hammond Hall quoted in *Building San Francisco's Parks: 1850–1930*, p. 68.

5. "Golden Gate Park: Coaxing the Barren Lands to Blossom as the Rose," *San Francisco Chronicle*, October 24, 1875, p. 2.

6. See Raymond Clary's two books, *The Making of Golden Gate Park, The Early Years: 1865–1906* and *The Making of Golden Gate Park, The Growing Years: 1906–1950*; and Christopher Pollock's *San Francisco's Golden Gate Park: A Thousand and Seventeen Acres of Stories.*

7. Angus Macfarlane has conducted extensive research on how the Sunset District got its name. See his two-part series "How the Sunset Became 'The Sunset'" (*Western Neighborhoods Project Newsletter*, Spring 2005, and online at http://www.outsidelands.org/sunset-name.php) and "The Sunset Finally Becomes Sunset" (*Western Neighborhoods Project Newsletter*, Winter 2007, and online at http://www.outsidelands.org/sunset-name2.php).

8. Members of this neighborhood group included "Julius Frankel, who had a ranch at Eleventh avenue and K street; Roy Keller, milk ranch at Nineteenth and K street; Bill Mahoney Sr., hog ranch at Fourteenth avenue and J street; Dick Burfiend, milk ranch near the old almshouse; Jim O'Brien, grading contractor; Jack Curley, grocer; Pat Furlong, who was proprietor of the 'Irish Tavern'; ... Jim Quigley and Frank Meadocraft, park gardeners," and others. "Club's Opposition to Laguna Honda Brings Change of Name for District," *San Francisco Chronicle*, April 25, 1925, p. 9T.

9. "Sunset District Cries for Relief," *San Francisco Call*, May 30, 1897, p. 30.

CHAPTER 4

THE SUNSET MEETS THE TWENTIETH CENTURY, 1890s–1920s

In the late nineteenth century, the Sunset was still dominated by sand dunes. Few streets were cut through, little housing had been built, so visitors were rare, except on the far east and far west of the district. In the 1890s, when the city's population had grown to more than 300,000, the Sunset District had fewer than 100 inhabitants, and few streets existed to help people get around and through the isolated area.

Looking northwest toward Nineteenth Avenue in 1900.

The only industries in the area were scattered dairies and gunpowder factories, which periodically exploded. Three workers died when the California Powder Works near the Central Ocean Road exploded on July 9, 1870. The factory exploded again in June 1872, December 1872 (killing two workers and seriously injuring three), and June 1877. The Giant Powder Works near 19th Avenue exploded in January 1879, and several workers died. These explosions went largely unnoticed when the sand dunes stood empty, but as more people began moving to the Sunset, more attention focused on the dangers of the gunpowder factories. As an 1879 newspaper wrote, "The explosion of the Giant Powder works … calls public attention to the danger which is inseparable to the existence of such works in populous neighborhoods. The Giant Powder works are near the Golden Gate Park, a place which has been set apart for recreation … If an explosion like that which occurred on Tuesday had taken place when the Park was largely occupied, no estimate can be made of the loss of life that might have resulted."[1] By 1880, gunpowder companies had left San Francisco.

In the late 1800s, a few Sunset homesteaders grew potatoes, barley, and other crops that thrive in a cold, foggy climate. The three largest "milk ranches" stood at what is now 10th Avenue and Lincoln Way, 7th Avenue and Lincoln Way, and 11th Avenue and Moraga Street. A 1932 *San Francisco Call Bulletin* article reminisced about the "famous milk shakes" people could get in earlier times at "The Milk Punch House … at 7th avenue, where the Laguna Honda School now is situated."[2]

Speculators, including Michael de Young, Charles Crocker, Fernando Nelson, and Adolph Sutro, were buying up land, convinced that the area would grow and flourish as a residential area. They were right, although the neighborhood's growth would not take hold until well into the twentieth century.

CARVILLE-BY-THE-SEA

As transit systems were electrifying their cars in the 1890s, horse-drawn streetcars and cable cars became obsolete. E. P. Vining, the general manager of San Francisco's Market Street Railroad, placed newspaper advertisements offering the old cars for sale: $20 for a car with seats and $10 for a car without seats. Adolph Sutro, who owned property along Ocean Beach, rented land to people who had bought these obsolete cars. Some cars became clubhouses for local groups; others provided vacation or even year-round housing.[3] The area was known as Carville-by-the-Sea, or Carville.

Obsolete streetcars were often dumped on the undeveloped Outer Sunset dunes.

By 1901 fifty families lived in car houses that sat from H to L Street and between 45th and 49th Avenues (now Lincoln Way to Lawton Street between 45th Avenue and the Great Highway). Some people stacked cars to form multistory car-buildings. Others placed three cars in a U shape to create a central courtyard. While some buildings combined a traditional structure with one or more streetcars, others were just cars with wheels removed and openings covered.

FOR SALE.

THE MARKET-STREET RAILWAY COMPANY, San Francisco, offers for sale a number of condemned

CAR BODIES.

PRICE WITHOUT SEATS, $10 EACH
OR WITH SEATS - - - $20 EACH
    Can be used for newsstands, fruitstands, lunchstands, offices, summer-houses, children's playhouses, poultry-houses, toolhouses, coalsheds, woodsheds, conservatories, rolling booths, etc. Apply to H. O. ROGERS, Division Superintendent, corner Fourth and Louisa streets, San Francisco.   MWF

The general manager of San Francisco's Market Street Railway found a unique way to dispose of obsolete horse-drawn streetcars through this newspaper ad.

Originally built in 1897 as the Vista del Mar, Carville's only hotel, this structure at 1338 47th Avenue became St. Andrew's Episcopal Church in the early 1900s.

In Carville people used obsolete horse-drawn streetcars and cable cars as homes and clubhouses.

Some streetcars and cablecars were stacked to form houses that were three stories high.

"We had lived in a car cottage first made out of three street cars and then two little bobtail cars put together for a living room. One faced west, we were on the west side of the street. One faced the ocean. That was my bedroom and my mother's. Another car faced the east. That was my grandma's bedroom. Then we had another car that faced the east for the kitchen. Facing south were two little bobtail cars with the partition taken out. That was our sitting room. ... There was a windmill for our own water right in front of this car cottage."

—

Myrtie Dickson in Patricia Turner, ed., *1906 Remembered*, p. 55

"'It took courage to come out here,' says Jules Getz of Sol Getz & Sons, pioneer beach real estate firm. 'We had a regular promotion program. We would advertise and people would ride out in their buggies. Most of them would scoff at us and tell us to peddle our sand somewhere else.'"

—

San Francisco News, April 10, 1947, p. 13

"At one point, my kid brother, Henry, bought a piece of property on 14th Avenue near Andronico's market. There were a lot of small houses around there then, and my brother was planning to put a house there. We started breaking walls down, and we suddenly heard glass break. Within the walls! So we took a couple of walls out and, my God, it was an old cable car!"

—

Andy Casper

Carville had a reputation for attracting a variety of people, often artistic, bohemian types. A "ladies' bicycle club," a card club, a café, and a hotel (later a church) all operated out of former streetcars and cable cars. Musicians met in a car they called La Bohème.

A 1938 article in the *San Francisco News* described Carville in 1900: "The little horsecar community was peacefully remote from bustling San Francisco ... the sand dunes behind it separated it from the residential area that had pushed its way through the bottleneck of hills."[4]

CARVILLE BECOMES OCEANSIDE BY THE 1920S

In the early twentieth century, developer Sol Getz bought blocks east of the Sutro land that hosted many of the Carville homes. In 1903, as Sol Getz & Sons began cutting through streets and grading them, Getz suggested renaming the neighborhood Oceanside. The City of San Francisco began installing streetlights, and Spring Valley Water Company began laying water mains.

Carville retained its popularity for a time after San Francisco's earthquake and fire in 1906. As more obsolete cars became available, displaced San Franciscans moved the cars out to the beach and joined the community of Carville. By 1908, almost 2,000 people had Carville homes, and the community hosted stores, restaurants, churches, hotels, and artistic clubs.

At the same time, though, many people moving to the Outside Lands wanted to live in more permanent homes. Developers like Sol Getz began buying lots near the beach and building conventional houses, which they lived in or offered for sale.

As the area became a more permanent residential community, the run-down streetcar homes were no longer welcome.

On July 4, 1913, Alexander Russell, president of the Oceanside Improvement Club, lit a bonfire igniting four (presumably empty) Carville houses to "burn the car out of Carville." (He had received permission from "Mrs. Merritt"—Adolph Sutro's daughter and heir—to set these cars on fire and had obtained a permit from the city to throw in a few fireworks.)[5] This action signaled the beginning of the end for the unique beachside community. Some residents stayed in their car-homes into the teens and early twenties, but by the mid-1920s the area had pretty much become the neighborhood of Oceanside. After Adolph Sutro's estate was finally settled in 1919 (he had died in 1898), the company Baldwin and Howell began selling his former land by the beach. A sales brochure headline read "From Carville to Real Homes."

By the mid-1920s the car-houses were gone, moved or destroyed, and increasingly replaced by permanent housing. Later the name Oceanside was dropped, as the area became part of the growing Sunset District. Only one former Carville house, made up of two cable cars and one horse car, remains on the beachside land that used to be Carville.

This aerial photograph of the Oceanside area in the early twentieth century shows increasing growth and development. The view looks southeast. The street running diagonally from the lower right of the photograph toward the dunes is Irving Street.

THE PARKSIDE

The Parkside District was one of the earliest sub-neighborhoods within the Sunset. Unlike Carville and Oceanside, the Parkside retains its original name. To this day, many residents do not consider the Parkside to be part of the larger Sunset District.

Parkside's boundaries are approximately Pacheco or Quintara Street on the north and Sigmund Stern Grove and Sloat Boulevard on the south. The eastern boundary follows the line of the previous San Miguel Rancho, at 12th and 15th Avenues north of Taraval Street and at 19th Avenue south of Taraval. The western boundary varies, depending on whom one talks to. Some people believe that Sunset Boulevard is the western boundary of the Parkside; others believe that the Parkside extends west to the ocean.

How was the area named? Like the rest of the city, the Sunset District had no tall trees and no developed parks. By the 1890s, the growing trees in Golden Gate Park had changed the sand dune topography, but the Parkside area was too far from Golden Gate Park for its name to refer to it.

A large group of trees grows in the southern part of the Parkside, on land now known as Sigmund Stern Grove and Pine Lake Park. The Green family, who lived on and farmed this land, began planting trees in the 1870s. By the turn of the century, tall trees towered over the area. Many people believe that the name Parkside came from the area's proximity to the Green property.

In 1900 few people lived in the Parkside. Parkside Realty Company was about to increase the number of residents.

Parkside Realty Company (PRC) formed in 1905, when William Crocker (son of Charles Crocker, one of the "Big Four" builders of the Transcontinental Railroad) and others began buying land in the Parkside, "a large real estate subdivision comprising nearly a fifth of the entire Sunset District."[6] PRC was formed to build homes and bring new residents to the Sunset sand dunes. It became apparent, however, that people would not buy those houses until streets were cut through and transit connected this area to the core of the city.

The area of dense trees in this photo was planted by George W. Green in the 1870s. The site is now Sigmund Stern Grove/Pine Lake Park. Sloat Boulevard runs to the right of the trees.

Unidentified representatives of Parkside Realty
Company pose in the sand dunes to advertise land
in the Parkside.

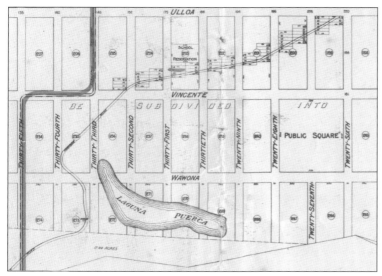

This early Parkside Realty Company
map shows that the early houses
between Ulloa and Vicente Streets
followed the Central Ocean Road, the
only street that ran through the Sunset
in the early 1900s.

This 1910 photo of the Parkside shows the dune plants growing close to new housing.

"I grew up in Glen Park. On Sundays we would visit my great-aunt at 15th and Santiago. We would look at new homes and play in the dunes."

—

Teresa Hurley

"West of 19th Avenue was just like wilderness back in the old days before the Parkside and Sunset Districts of San Francisco were heavily populated. There were literally thousands of jack rabbits, squirrels, and the like roaming among the high dune grasses and wildflowers of the undulating hills which stretched all the way to the beach. … Hunting was not just a sport at that time. Many people looked forward to the wild rabbits, which they were able to capture, to be part of their dinner."

—

Mary Ada Williams,
More Parkside Pranks and Sunset Stunts,
p. 78

"When we moved into that house on 18th Avenue there were only four other homes in that block. There were no streets or sidewalks—it was really country. Between our place at 18th and Noriega and the beach there were less than 100 homes. It was all open land and a big hill where we hunted pheasants and cottontail rabbits."

—

Stan Adair (born 1919)

In 1908, when United Railroads was running a streetcar line along H Street (now Lincoln Way) to the beach, and the 17 line ran along 20th Avenue (see pages 36 and 89), Parkside Realty Company began building homes. The houses appear to have been systematically built along the route of the Central Ocean Road, which was the only street in the area at that time. Some of PRC's houses still stand, clustered near a route that no longer exists amid the familiar street grid that we know today.

Rosemary (Trodden) French (front right) lived on Laguna Street. She and her family visited the Parkside on weekends in the 1920s.

This Parkside Realty Company home still stands on 31st Avenue. These houses were built without garages, as most people did not own automobiles in the early 1900s. Almost all of the extant PRC houses have been raised to accommodate garages.

A CITY SCHOOL BECOMES A CHURCH, 1917

In 1909 San Francisco opened the first Parkside School, a one-room schoolhouse on Taraval Street near 31st Avenue. After the school closed in 1917, San Francisco Mayor James Rolph donated the building to the Catholic archdiocese to help build the St. Cecilia parish. The archdiocese moved the building to 15th and Taraval, enlarged it, and reopened it as the first St. Cecilia Church. Today it is difficult to imagine a mayor donating a public building to a religious group.

The original Parkside School (above) was a one-room building. The Archdiocese of San Francisco remodeled and added to the original Parkside School to create the first St. Cecilia Church (at right).

The new Parkside Elementary School on 25th Avenue in the 1920s. The building was razed in the late 1990s.

"My family lost its home south of Market during the earthquake and fire of 1906. My aunts' friend, a contractor, said, 'Why don't you buy a lot out there in the Sunset?' My aunts said, 'Oh, Lord. There's no one out there. There's nothing but sand.' And he said, 'That's true now, but you'd be surprised. A lot of people are doing very well moving out there.' My aunts bought a lot on 6th Avenue above Irving. They built flats, and the whole family lived there."

—

Catherine Murphy
(born 1914)

"I was born in 1920 and grew up at 274 Parnassus Avenue at Fourth Avenue. There were few houses past Ninth Avenue. My mother had a car. She called it 'the machine' and would drive us children to the beach. There were lupines in the sand. My sister and I collected ladybugs."

—

Jeanne Warden
(born 1920)

"The small grocery stores didn't have names. They'd call them by the name of the owner. Ours was Schwaderer's, which had the first telephone on our street. Mr. Schwaderer knew that my mother sent a postcard to her sister every day. When the mailman came, Schwaderer would say, 'Don't forget to pick up the mail. She has that postcard to go out.' And if my mother went out, Schwaderer had a key that fit our house. We could always borrow the key from him to get into our home."

—

Catherine Murphy
(born 1914)

THE INNER SUNSET AND GOLDEN GATE HEIGHTS

The boundaries of the Inner Sunset are Lincoln Way on the north, 19th Avenue on the west, and Ortega or Pacheco on the south. The eastern boundary is less clear. Just south of Golden Gate Park, Arguello Street serves as the eastern boundary, but this street runs for only two blocks before dead-ending at the parking lot below the University of California Medical Center. The Inner Sunset does not include the U.C. Medical Center (which is in Parnassus Heights), Golden Gate Heights, Forest Hill, or West Portal. Its eastern boundary zigzags around these other western neighborhoods. Bordering the already developed Haight-Ashbury District, the Inner Sunset became one of the early areas of the Sunset to experience population growth.

Catherine Murphy lived on Kirkham near 12th Avenue when she was a child. She remembers that few people lived there and neighbors were friendly. She recalls, "If my mother sat on the front steps, she'd see all the people going to the grocery store. And they became friends. Theirs was a greeting-and-talking friendship. People would give you the news of what happened here or there in the Sunset."

By 1908, the Inner Sunset was still largely unpopulated. The steam cloud at the top left of the photograph comes from a water pumping station in Golden Gate Park.

Golden Gate Heights is an unusual sub-neighborhood that sits atop the hills on the eastern edge of the Sunset. Its boundaries were described in 1925 as "on a knoll, well out of the sand dunes, but still in the Sunset district, running from 11th to 17th avenue and from Kirkham to Quintara street."[7]

This aerial view shows the developed areas around the hills of Golden Gate Heights just east of the main Sunset District. City engineer Michael O'Shaughnessy began grading the streets and building stairways on this steep hillside in 1928.

The San Francisco Department of Public Works built stairways on the hills of Golden Gate Heights to help pedestrians walk on the steep, often muddy hills.

Many Golden Gate Heights houses have striking western views of the Sunset District and the ocean. The area was wild and mountainous until the Department of Public Works graded it and built the roads in 1928. Originally, streets were planned in the familiar San Francisco grid pattern, but city engineer Michael O'Shaughnessy realized that the hills were too steep and decided to build streets that conformed to the contours of the hills. Some streets that run parallel elsewhere—for example, 14th and 15th Avenues, and Noriega and Ortega Streets—intersect in Golden Gate Heights. Builders also created stairways for pedestrians navigating the steep hills.

San Francisco built the roads and stairways of Golden Gate Heights in the late 1920s, but the beginning of the Great Depression in 1929 prevented most building in the neighborhood until after World War II. Most of the buildings were erected in the 1950s and later. The area is a hodgepodge of buildings from different eras and with differing styles.

"As late as the early 1970s, when we moved to Golden Gate Heights, the area still had a variety of wild animals. I remember two foxes and the European lady who came every morning with her two dogs to feed them chicken. I was always surprised when the foxes weren't afraid of the dogs. Within five years of our moving here, houses were built and the foxes were gone."

—

Barbara Meli

"I realize we can't stop progress, and villages grow to be towns, towns grow to be cities, and cities grow to be metropolises. But underneath all that growth is the sadness that comes with houses side by side without an inch in between; the disappearance of the grove of trees where we kids camped out, free from fear; and the small-town atmosphere where we never locked our doors—to the bars on the windows to keep bad guys from breaking into the homes. All that's left are memories."

—

Stan Adair (born 1919)

"There we all were, living in the Sunset not realizing at the time how nice it was to dwell there. Only after moving away did we come to appreciate the virtues of the good old neighborhood."

—

Steve Aguado, *Sunset Memories*, p. 1

This house on 14th Avenue was, in 1939, one of the first houses built in Golden Gate Heights.

Streets were still being built in Golden Gate Heights in 1930.

As late as the 1970s, Barbara Meli regularly saw a family of foxes in this area of Golden Gate Heights.

THE BURNHAM PLAN, 1905

On January 15, 1904, a group of San Franciscans formed the Association for the Improvement and Adornment of San Francisco. One of the association's first actions was to hire Daniel H. Burnham to design a plan for the growth of San Francisco.[8] A well-known Chicago architect and city planner, Burnham was part of the popular City Beautiful movement, which stressed the importance of planning the growth of cities so that they were not simply practical and efficient but also attractive. When he came to San Francisco, Burnham had already created plans for Washington, D.C., Cleveland, and Chicago.

Burnham and his assistant, Edward Bennett, traveled to San Francisco in 1904 and completed the Burnham Plan for San Francisco in 1905. Burnham wrote that his plan was not to reflect "what the city is, so much as what it is to be."

The Burnham Plan featured large parks ("public squares"), numerous playgrounds, wide diagonal boulevards, and a large outdoor amphitheater. It also called for a boulevard to surround the city and an extension of the Golden Gate Park panhandle to Van Ness Avenue. James Phelan, president of the Association for the Improvement and Adornment of San Francisco, wrote, "What the people have needed is an ideal with which to nourish their imagination and to give them a goal towards which to labor with confidence. That they have in the Burnham Plan."[9]

People who know of the Burnham Plan often know only of its proposals for other areas of the city. However, Burnham wanted to make changes in the western side of San Francisco as well. In the Sunset, Burnham proposed breaking up the grid pattern with diagonal streets and a large public square covering the entire block from 34th to 35th Avenue between Pacheco and Quintara. The proposal included building a large parkway running east to west from Twin Peaks to the beach. Burnham also recommended widening 19th Avenue, probably the only part of the Burnham Plan that was eventually implemented in the Sunset.

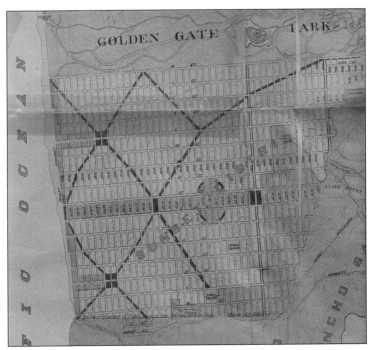

Daniel Burnham suggested that wide boulevards, diagonal streets, and additional parks be built in the Sunset District.

Enthusiasm for Burnham's ideas was interrupted by the 1906 earthquake and fire. In the rush to rebuild San Francisco after this disaster, the city paid little attention to the Burnham Plan.

The 1906 Earthquake and Fire

The eastern part of San Francisco was in ruins after the 1906 earthquake and fire.

Early in the morning of April 18, 1906, San Francisco was jolted by a major earthquake followed by a devastating fire that left more than 200,000 people homeless. Few buildings stood in the Sunset; damage and injuries were much less severe there than in other areas of the city. The fire that destroyed the core of San Francisco stopped more than two miles east of the neighborhood.

Clarence E. Judson gave a firsthand account of being at Ocean Beach at the time:

> I got up to take my usual dip in the surf. … I started to go out, and instantly there came such a shock. I was thrown to my knees. I got up and was down again. I was dazed and stunned, and being tossed about by the breakers, my ears full of salt water and about a gallon in my stomach. I was thrown down three times, and only by desperate fighting did I get out at all.
>
> … I tried to run to where my shoes, hat, and bath robe lay. … I thought of lightning, as the beach was full of phosphorus. Every step I took left a brilliant incandescent streak. I jumped on my bath robe to save me. … I reached for my shoes and landed with both feet onto my hat, twice. I finally got dressed after being thrown to the ground a few more times. … When I got to the new road up on the sand dunes [the Great Highway] I saw the road was badly cracked, houses were out of plumb, men, women and children were coming out in the streets, dogs were barking and chickens cackling.[10]

Josephine Baxter, who lived on the 1300 block of 9th Avenue, wrote a long letter to her parents in Omaha, Nebraska, to tell them about the events during and following the 1906 earthquake. She wrote:

> Baby woke and I gave her a bottle and she started off to sleep when that awful shock came at 5:15 (A.M.). … every shake seemed as if the house would be torn away. I can never describe or forget that horrible minute. It seemed an eternity. … We went over to Dr. McFarlane's [1217 19th Avenue; house at 802 I Street] … You ought to have seen their new drug store; scarcely a bottle remained on the shelf. … I never saw such looking rooms … It was a wonder the children did not get hurt. … The next morning … people were passing our house in all sorts of rigs and every face was terror stricken. … the people in every conceivable rig and outfit streamed by our house all day and night, camping every where. Non slept—such a tired looking people. Many had walked out all the way from town, for the safest place in the city was this part, north and south of the Park.[11]

Two structures in the Sunset District suffered damage from the earthquake: the new St. Anne of the Sunset Catholic church (built 1905) and the Olympic Grounds. The church suffered some damage, but parishioners continued to use the building until the new church was built more than twenty years later. The Olympic Grounds, a sports facility owned by the Olympic Club, stood in the near-empty dunes on 7th Avenue in the Inner Sunset. When it opened in 1890, it was "one of the finest track facilities in the world."[12] It had a 16-mile running track, a 135-yard straight track, handball court, and a 3,000-seat grandstand. The earthquake damaged most of the Olympic Grounds facilities, and only the handball court remained, as the surrounding areas began to be covered with housing.

"The quake didn't bother me at all, out here on 47th Avenue between Judah and Kirkham. We had lived in a car cottage first. … Six months before the earthquake, we built a house and moved in there the end of October. When the earthquake came the following April, the 18th, we were living there. But we weren't bothered at all. … It woke me up. … I got up and I fell down. … but we had almost no damage."

—

Myrtie Dickson, quoted in Patricia Turner, ed., *1906 Remembered*, p. 55

"When Shorty Roberts's daughters Agnes and Isabel were young, they were bored living so far out, away from the city. They were excited in 1906 when many people began camping out in the sand dunes after the earthquake and fire."

—

Alex Spotorno,
grand-nephew of Shorty Roberts

After the 1906 earthquake and fire, more people began looking for housing in the less-crowded Outside Lands. All those years of buying land in the Sunset began to pay off for speculators, as construction of streets and housing began in earnest. But first came one of the most significant after-effects of the earthquake in the Sunset District: a bribery/graft trial that involved the Parkside Realty Company and Abraham Ruef.

"Boss" Abe Ruef

Abraham ("Abe") Ruef was born in San Francisco in 1864. After earning a degree in classics at the University of California, Berkeley, he attended Hastings College of the Law and became an attorney in 1886. One of his clients was Eugene Schmitz, president of the local musicians' union. Ruef persuaded Schmitz to run for mayor; with Ruef's help, Schmitz won the election in 1901 and was reelected in 1903 and 1905.

Before long, Ruef (known as "Boss Ruef") was one of the most influential people in city government. He never held elected office, but he received large fees from many businesses for "legal consultation" or "protection." He often passed on part of these fees to the mayor and other politicians. At one time, most members of the San Francisco Board of Supervisors (which then had eighteen members) received bribes from Ruef for their votes on certain issues.

Abraham Ruef, 1928.

The Sunset played a part in Ruef's activities because it was a growing area where city government attention was needed. In early 1906, Parkside Realty Company (PRC) formed the Parkside Transit Company, which applied to the board of supervisors for a franchise to build a streetcar line (the #17) along 20th Avenue. PRC also approached Mayor Schmitz, who showed interest in opening up the Parkside to housing and expressed support for the streetcar line. Based on the mayor's encouragement, the PRC began to transform the sand dunes of 20th Avenue by building the streets and laying utility lines. PRC also invited members of the board of supervisors to tour the Parkside and learn more about the housing planned for the area. During a luncheon following this tour, Supervisor Charles Boxton was remembered for making what became known as the black flag speech: "… we are the city fathers. … it must be borne in mind that without the city fathers there can be no public service corporations. The street cars cannot run, lights cannot be furnished, telephones cannot exist. … we, the city fathers … are not in business for our health. The question at this banquet board is: 'How much money is in it for us?'"[13]

Probably recognizing the great power Ruef held in city decision-making, Parkside Realty Company decided to approach him. According to Ruef biographer Walton Bean, the PRC used Gus H. Umbsen, whose company would sell the Parkside properties, to hire Ruef as its attorney, offering the great fee of $30,000 over two years. The board of supervisors approved the franchise in March 1906. After the 1906 earthquake in April, Umbsen supposedly paid half of the fee ($15,000) to Ruef, who indicated that he would pay each member of the board of supervisors $750 for a favorable vote, although these payments were never made.

By 1906, the graft in city government had become public. One trial involved the Parkside Transit Company franchise, and another Sunset connection occurred after months of delays orchestrated by Ruef's attorneys. Ruef was granted bail on March 4, 1907, but was told to report to the court the next day. Instead, he "went into hiding" at the Trocadero Inn, a roadhouse in today's Sigmund Stern Grove. He was found at the Trocadero on March 8 and began to face his accusers in court on March 11. A grand jury indicted Mayor Schmitz and Abe Ruef for extortion and bribery. Ultimately, the grand jury returned more than ninety indictments against Abe Ruef.

At the Parkside Realty Company trial, J. E. Green of the realty company refused to testify on the grounds that he might incriminate himself. When the prosecutor dropped the fourteen charges against him, Green testified against Ruef. Umbsen was granted immunity and also testified against Ruef. Still, the jury was deadlocked, six to six, and Ruef was found not guilty in the PRC case.

The prosecution then proceeded with the other charges against Ruef. The various graft trials removed the mayor and members of the board of supervisors from office. Abe Ruef was the only person who went to prison; he was sentenced to fourteen years at San Quentin Prison and served almost five years before being paroled. (No one who may have actually paid the bribes was ever convicted; few, if any, were even prosecuted.)

The new board of supervisors approved the streetcar line on 20th Avenue because "it was considered so important and necessary for the city's development."[14]

The 17 streetcar line ran on 20th Avenue when this photograph was taken in 1914.

STREET RENAMING, 1909

By 1908 the U.S. Post Office was complaining about duplicate streets in San Francisco, estimating that 500 letters were delivered to the wrong addresses each day. Sunset streets running north to south were numbered avenues and were often confused with numbered avenues in the Bayview District, which had a "South" designation (e.g., 26th Avenue South). (Today, people are sometimes still confused by the difference between, for example, 9th Street downtown and 9th Avenue in the western part of the city.) In 1908, there were no zip codes or other ways to make a distinction between similarly named streets.

Streets running east to west in the Sunset and Richmond Districts had been assigned alphabetical letters. A through D streets ran through the Richmond, north of Golden Gate Park; H through X streets ran south of the park.

In 1908 the San Francisco Board of Supervisors appointed a special commission to consider renaming streets throughout the city.[15] The commission recommended retaining the alphabetical order of east-west streets in the Richmond and Sunset Districts but renaming them after Spanish explorers and early California settlers.

When Sunset residents heard about the plan, they objected, saying they did not live in "Spanish Town." The final change was a compromise, giving Spanish names to some streets, exchanging some names with those

Sunset residents initially opposed the street renaming in 1909 because the new street names were almost all Spanish in origin. The cartoon above, drawn by Oscar Chopin, appeared in the *San Francisco Chronicle* on November 23, 1909. The man in the background is Mayor Edward Robson Taylor.

originally considered for other districts, and allowing some street names originated by Parkside Realty Company to prevail. In the Richmond District, the new street names were Anza, Balboa, and Cabrillo. D Street had already become Fulton when that street was extended to the neighborhood. E, F, and G Streets never really existed; they would have run on property that became Golden Gate Park.

In the Sunset, H Street was renamed Lincoln Way, commemorating the 100th anniversary of President Abraham Lincoln's birth. I through O streets became Irving, Judah, Kirkham, Lawton, Moraga, Noriega, and Ortega. For P through W streets, the city adopted the names already being used by the Parkside Realty Company: Pacheco, Quintara, Rivera, Santiago, Taraval, Ulloa, Vicente, and Wawona. X Street might have become Xavier, but people considered the name too difficult to pronounce, so X was skipped, the letter was changed to Y, and the street became Yorba. The only numbered street whose name was changed was First Avenue, which became Arguello Boulevard. (In 1923, 13th Avenue was renamed Funston after Brigadier General Frederick Funston.)

Some Sunset residents wonder about Hugo Street, which runs between Lincoln Way and Irving Street, from Arguello to 7th Avenue. Early maps drawn in the mid-1800s do not include this street, but Hugo does appear on maps in the 1890s. Popular folklore mentions author Victor Hugo as the inspiration for this street name; however, another source of the name may be more realistic. Adolph Sutro owned this land, and around 1892 he had the new street, Hugo, cut through between H and I Streets. Recent research conducted by local historian Angus Macfarlane revealed that Adolph had a brother in Germany named Hugo, so the street may well have been named after him.

ROADHOUSES

In the late 1800s, the Sunset's western edge was known for its hotels, bars, and restaurants—often called roadhouses. People could leave the central part of San Francisco and head toward the beach "suburbs" to enjoy drinking, dancing, and partying. Many of the roadhouses served alcohol during Prohibition and possibly offered other "non-respectable" activities.

However, not all of these roadhouses had bad reputations. Two of the best-known Sunset destinations were Roberts Family Resort (Roberts-at-the-Beach) and Oceanside House (later Tait's-at-the-Beach). Neither business still stands, but both have interesting histories.

Dominic Roberts bought the Seabreeze Resort in 1895. He later renamed it Roberts Family Resort.

Dominic (Shorty) Roberts moved to San Francisco from Malta in 1895. Two years later, he bought the Seabreeze Resort at 2200 Great Highway. He remodeled and reopened the business as Roberts Family Resort, which became a popular destination for many San Franciscans.

Every year the Roberts Family Resort hosted the Bear Barbecue. Local legend says that bear meat was served at Bear Barbecue, but according to Roberts's grandnephew, Alex Spotorno, "Shorty had a pet bear on a chain with a collar. That's where the Bear Barbecue name came from."[16]

After Shorty Roberts died in 1912, his eldest son, Richie (also known as Shorty), owned and ran the popular Cliff House for a short time but closed it during Prohibition. Then he began running Roberts Family Resort (later Roberts-at-the-Beach) with his brother. The inn, located where the Seabreeze had been, survived Prohibition ("no one was remembered to have gone thirsty"), although the *San Francisco Chronicle* reported that it was raided in May 1930: "Agents did not arrest any of the 650 guests, but seized alcohol."

"Shorty Roberts's son, my uncle Richie (also called Shorty), made a go of running the famed Cliff House. It had closed around World War I for two years. He remodeled it and reopened it in 1920, but because of Prohibition, he closed it in 1925. Then he began running Roberts-at-the-Beach with his brother Wilfred."

—

Alex Spotorno

"I used to ride Blackie when I was twelve or thirteen years old. He was kept at the stable my family started on 48th Avenue."

—

Alex Spotorno

"As a child in the 1930s, I heard rumors that after dark, certain buildings along the beach housed gambling houses and brothels. I had the impression that Ocean Beach, because of its isolation, was a safer place than the Tenderloin or Fillmore District for prominent citizens to patronize brothels."

—

Dorothy Bryant

Roberts-at-the-Beach was *the* place to go from the 1920s to the 1950s. Over the years, guests included C. S. Howard (owner of the racehorse Seabiscuit), Mayors James Rolph and Angelo Rossi, columnist Herb Caen, and entertainer Bing Crosby. Customers enjoyed chicken loaf, terrapin stew, "steak à la cliff," and other popular delicacies.

Shorty Roberts appeared in local newspapers after his twelve-year-old horse, Blackie, swam across San Francisco Bay from Marin County to San Francisco's Crissy Field on October 1, 1938. Roberts had entered into a $1,000 bet with Bill Kyne, of the Bay Meadows racetrack, who had said that horses could not swim.[17]

Shorty accompanied the horse on the swim. According to Alex Spotorno, Shorty's nephew, "Wetsuits were pretty much unheard of at the time, so Shorty covered his body with grease to protect him from the cold water. Shorty couldn't swim, so he wore a life preserver and held onto Blackie's tail." The swim took twenty-three minutes and fifteen seconds. When Blackie and Shorty arrived on the San Francisco shore, oats and hay were waiting for Blackie, but he turned around and headed back toward the water. Shorty always insisted that the horse loved swimming in the bay.

Blackie, "the wonder horse," swam across San Francisco Bay with Shorty Roberts in tow.

Shorty Roberts cooked popular meals at the "fireplace broiler."

The evening after the swim, Roberts-at-the-Beach had a huge party to celebrate Blackie's accomplishment. The swim was a popular story in all the newspapers the next day and was frequently repeated in San Francisco papers through the 1980s.[18]

The Roberts-at-the-Beach nightclub and restaurant closed in 1955, but the owners continued to cater parties and weddings until 1966. At one point the family opened a Roberts Motel at 2828 Sloat Boulevard, but it never enjoyed the popularity of the original restaurant and hotel.

Another roadhouse with an interesting history was the popular Oceanside House (or Tait's-at-the-Beach) on the Great Highway between Ulloa and Vicente Streets. The building was originally constructed in the 1850s as a mansion for attorney Bela Brooks. The residence was sold in the 1860s and later opened as Oceanside House. When the roadhouse closed around 1900, the building became a home once again, this time to Ida and Alexander Russell, who are credited with bringing the concepts of Zen Buddhism to mainstream America.[19] After the Russells sold the building in 1920, it reverted to a roadhouse, this time called Tait's-at-the-Beach.

San Francisco Chronicle columnist Millie Robbins wrote in her column, "Countless prominent personalities of the period, including a couple of U.S. Presidents, dined within this weathered wooden building. The food was excellent, the service good, the bands played danceable music, and the atmosphere, though subdued, wasn't starchy."[20] In 2002, Matthew Brady wrote in *The Independent* that in the 1860s and 1870s, Oceanside House "was the only place for good cheer" on the western side of San Francisco.[21]

Tait's closed in 1931. The building stood empty until it was destroyed by fire in 1940.

Over the years, this grand building on the Great Highway was home to Bela Brooks and the Russells and open to the public as Oceanside House and Tait's-at-the-Beach.

On August 31, 1902, the *Call* newspaper announced a contest, asking subscribers to estimate the number of people who would vote in the upcoming gubernatorial election. The first prize was a $5,000 house and lot in the Sunset District, "San Francisco's most popular and attractive section." The image on the left accompanied the article, which said that the house was located "one block from Golden Gate Park and one block south of the Park's new entrance via the Ninteenth-avenue boulevard."

ADVOCATING FOR THE NEIGHBORHOOD

As the twentieth century got under way, Sunset "pioneers" appealed to the city for amenities such as paved streets, telephone service, streetlights, public transportation, postal service, and schools. Often these requests fell on deaf ears. The area was still considered a remote suburb; to most people, Sunset District events happened "outside San Francisco" or "seven miles from San Francisco."

One of the most active local groups was the Parkside Improvement Club. Within a year of its founding in 1908, this neighborhood group was successful "in having several street lights installed, telephone service made available, a volunteer fire department established, daily mail delivery to mail boxes along T (Taraval) Street, a double streetcar track on T Street, … a school of four grades, and a concrete sewer for the district." The club also advocated for tunnels to connect the area with downtown San Francisco; the Twin Peaks Tunnel opened in 1918 and the Sunset Tunnel opened in 1928. (See chapter 7.)

Another group, the Sunset Transportation and Development Association, supported a 1930s proposal to build a firebreak in the Sunset, a new road running diagonally from the zoo and children's playground at the western end of Sloat Boulevard through the Sunset to Lincoln Way. Called Sunset Boulevard, the road was reminiscent of streets proposed in the Daniel Burnham Plan of 1905. That Sunset Boulevard was never built; today's Sunset Boulevard was at that time called Parkside Drive.

SLOW GROWTH

In the twentieth century, as public transportation lines spread to the area and the use of the automobile increased, new houses made living in the Sunset more attractive to families. A Sunset building boom began in the 1930s. While building elsewhere slowed down during the Great Depression, construction in the Sunset continued. Building stopped almost completely, though, during World War II and picked up again after 1945. By 1970, the Sunset, once called a suburb of San Francisco, was a thriving neighborhood with all the original sand dunes covered.

Rabbit hunting was a popular pastime in the Parkside in 1915.

By the 1930s, the Inner Sunset and the Richmond District (upper part of photo) had been developed, but Golden Gate Heights had very few houses, and streets were still being built.

Mark Rivero (left, standing) and his family in the 1920s across from his home on Lawton Street between 22nd and 23rd Avenues.

NOTES

1. *Daily Morning Call*, January 16, 1879, p. 2.

2. *San Francisco Call Bulletin*, April 29, 1932.

3. For the best description and images of Carville, see Woody LaBounty, *Carville-by-the-Sea: San Francisco's Streetcar Suburb*.

4. "Air Views of San Francisco," *San Francisco News,* February 3, 1938, p. 19.

5. "Burn the Car Out of 'Carville,' Residents of Oceanside Celebrate," *San Francisco Chronicle,* July 6, 1913, p. 38.

6. Walton Bean, *Boss Ruef's San Francisco,* p. 90.

7. "Golden Gate Heights Owners Pool Holding to Improve Region," *San Francisco Chronicle,* April 25, 1925, p. 6T.

8. For information and commentary about Daniel Burnham's complete plan for San Francisco, see Edward F. O'Day, ed., *Report on a Plan for San Francisco by Daniel Burnham*; Judd Kahn, *Imperial San Francisco;* and Joan E. Draper, *Edward H. Bennett: Architect and City Planner, 1874–1954.*

9. Edward F. O'Day, ed., *Report on a Plan for San Francisco by Daniel H. Burnham,* p. 209.

10, Clarence E. Judson, quoted in *Denial of Disaster*, by Gladys Hansen and Emmet Condon, pp. 29–30.

11. Josephine (Fearon) Baxter, "1906 San Francisco Earthquake, Copy of Letter to Her Parents in Omaha, Nebraska, Covering Period Tuesday, April 17, to Monday, April 23."

12. Ronald Fimrite, *The Olympic Club of San Francisco 1860–2009*, p. 50.

13. Walton Bean, *Boss Ruef's San Francisco*, pp. 93–94.

14. Ibid., p. 277.

15. For articles on the changing of street names in 1909, see John Freeman's "Spanish Town: Street Names in Western San Francisco" online at http://www.outsidelands.org/street-names.php and "Street Naming Controversy—1909" in the Encyclopedia of San Francisco at http://www.sfhistoryencyclopedia.com/articles/s/streetNaming.html.

16. From an interview with Alex Spotorno, nephew of Shorty Roberts, June 26, 2004.

17. This account of the Blackie story appears online at http://www.outsidelands.org/blackie.php.

18. Roberts's Blackie is often confused with a Tiburon swayback horse that is immortalized in a statue in "Blackie's Pasture," but they were different horses.

19. For more information about the building and about Ida and Alexander Russell, see Woody LaBounty's article "Tait's-at-the-Beach: The House of Mystery," online at http://www.outsidelands.org/sw21.php.

20. Millie Robbins, *Tales of Love and Hate in Old San Francisco* (a collection of newspaper columns), p. 152.

21. Matthew Brady, "The Champagne Posse," *San Francisco Independent,* March 5, 2002, p. 14a.

CHAPTER 5

HOME BUILDERS COVER
THE DUNES, 1920s–1940s

"The settlers of San Francisco settled around the bay, close to where the ships found shelter. San Francisco started as a small village forty-two years ago. It has constantly grown, and taken its way westward. Little did the early settlers dream that the city would in their day extend almost to the ocean; but it has grown and it will keep on growing. I hope that in ten years more you will see solid rows of houses extending all the way to the beach."

—Adolph Sutro, quoted in the
San Francisco Call, February 3, 1892

It took far longer than the ten years Sutro hoped it would take for builders to transform the sand dunes of the Sunset District into the residential neighborhood we know today: gridded streets with look-alike houses that have garages on the ground floor and living space above. (This type of building, common in San Francisco, is now identified as unsafe in earthquakes, when a "soft story"—a garage or storefront on the ground floor—is more vulnerable to collapse unless properly braced.)

Building in the central Sunset began in the late 1920s, with the majority of the houses built in the 1930s and 1940s. Most building stopped during World War II but started again after the war ended in 1945.

BUILDING A NEIGHBORHOOD

The best-known builders in the Sunset were Henry Doelger, Carl and Fred Gellert, R. F. Galli, and Oliver Rousseau. Builders borrowed designs and details from one another, such as varying entrances (outside stairs, covered stairs, tunnel), patios outside the dining room, and similar floor plans. It is not always easy to identify which developer built which houses.

An important difference between these builders and the "developers" of today is that Doelger and others were individual entrepreneurs who built in neighborhoods where they and their families would live. Today's developers are often corporations that exist elsewhere, build a subdivision, and then move on. In contrast, the Sunset builders had a personal stake in creating good housing and neighborhoods. Doelger and his family lived on 15th Avenue while he was building in the Sunset (and later in Daly City when he was building there). The Gallis lived on 28th Avenue and later on 23rd Avenue, and the Rousseaus lived on 36th Avenue—all in houses that the family patriarch had built in or near the neighborhoods he was creating.

Small, lesser-known builders also constructed houses throughout the Sunset District, some one or two at a time. These builders often bought single lots on already-developed blocks and built custom homes for individual buyers.

Sunset houses were often criticized for their similarity and lack of diverse details, but they enabled working-class families to attain the American dream of home ownership, once available only to the wealthy. Until these small houses were built, most working-class families lived in rented apartments, often substandard, in the densely populated eastern parts of San Francisco. A house in the Sunset meant an escape from this way of life—and often meant better schools and living conditions for children.

Many Sunset houses had the same floor plan as most nearby houses, with the garage on the street level and the living quarters above. Each house had two strips of lawn in front, although most subsequent owners have paved over the lawns with concrete.

Many Sunset builders "presented" model homes—furnished houses that prospective buyers could visit before deciding to buy. With modern furniture and other "extras" from Lachman Bros., Sterling Furniture Company, Frank Newman Co., and Redlick-Newman Co., builders hoped to make the model houses attractive to buyers.

"People would look at a model house, then pick one under construction that they wanted to buy," said Ray Galli Jr. "I think that was new at the time, at least for San Francisco. Before that, many builders just built one home at a time."[1]

To attract buyers, Sunset builders gave names to groups of houses, including the American, the Styleocrat, Sunstream Homes, and Casa Moderna. Builders used other sales techniques, offering low down payments and FHA payment terms (starting in the 1930s, during the Great Depression) and restricting sales to Caucasians, considered the hallmark of a wealthy neighborhood in those days. (See chapter 9.)

During the 1930s, some property owners lost money and had to sell off Sunset land. One newspaper ad promoted lots on 46th and 47th Avenues: "'Help Yourself' Sale of Choice Sunset Lots Sacrificed for Cash! Owner has just opened entire block. Come and choose."[2] Builders with money could buy Sunset land at lower prices.

During World War II, when building materials were harder to obtain, some builders concentrated on "war housing," smaller houses designed for people who worked in the factories and other industries that supported the war. Some of these houses built by R. F. Galli still stand on 45th Avenue between Quintara and Rivera Streets. When the war ended, the builders returned to building larger homes in San Francisco or in other Bay Area communities.

The living room of a Sunset house on 27th Avenue between Moraga and Noriega Streets in about 1937.

A typical newspaper ad of the early 1940s advertising the builder, describing a model home and the company that provided the interior furnishings, and promoting the reasonable cost and "FHA Terms."

"When I was growing up, we lived on the 2200 block of 33rd Avenue. Lindsay built our home. My father bought it when it was new and was very satisfied with it. It had the brand-new innovation: the inside patio. We had a tunnel entrance. Beautiful stairs. Tile. It looked like a Mexican staircase. It was really nice."

—

Andy Casper (born 1924)

"Lindsay was one of the first San Francisco builders to utilize the skylight extensively."

—

San Francisco Chronicle,
September 8, 1940

"Louie Epp looked like a carpenter working for somebody else. When I first saw him, he was wearing white overalls with a hat pulled down to his ears, a cigar butt in his mouth, carrying a hammer. We put in an order for two houses, one for my husband and me and one for my sister and her husband. I believe that those houses launched Louie's contracting work. He eventually built eighteen houses on this street and showed his appreciation for me by doing all kinds of things. Everything extra I asked for, he'd say, 'It'll cost you,' and I'd say, 'That's all right, Louie.' But when we came to pay him, he didn't charge me for any of those extras."

—

Marie McCormack (born 1907)

BUILDING ONE HOUSE AT A TIME

Many small builders bought single lots here and there and built houses one at a time. These builders included Louis "Louie" Epp, Sol Getz (Getz & Sons), Oscar Heyman & Brothers, Lang Realty Company, Claude T. "C. T." Lindsay, James "Jimmy" McDonagh, Chris McKeon (Happy Homes), Gus Moeller, Fernando Nelson & Sons, and Fred Warden.

C. T. Lindsay built this house on 35th Avenue in 1940.

Louis Epp built this house on 34th Avenue.

James "Jimmy" McDonagh

Jimmy McDonagh was born in Ireland in 1914. In 1948, he and his family moved to San Francisco, where he worked on a variety of construction projects.[3]

The McDonagh family lived in an apartment on 11th Avenue between Kirkham and Judah Streets until he could afford to buy a lot at 739 Kirkham Street. He built his house on that lot in 1953 and lived there until a few years before his death.

A McDonagh apartment building on 8th Avenue.

In 1957 McDonagh formed a partnership with Joseph Driscoll. For the next two years, Driscoll and McDonagh built on existing vacant lots or demolished existing buildings and built houses and apartment buildings. Instead of selling their buildings, they often rented out the units they built.

"The flats and apartment buildings that Jimmy and his fellow developers built were commonly known as 'Richmond or Sunset specials,'" explains McDonagh's son Steve. "The architecture was nothing special—they were simple, and so were the insides."

Jimmy McDonagh died in September 1974.

Chris McKeon

Chris McKeon was born in San Francisco and raised in the Mission District. As a young man, he worked for his family's meatpacking firm. He entered construction in 1927. His first houses were near McLaren Park, and then he began building in the Sunset. His sales office, Happy Homes Building Company, stood at 948 Taraval Street (at 20th), and he lived at 345 Santiago Street.

A row of Chris McKeon's houses in the Parkside District.

McKeon built houses on various Sunset lots, including on 35th Avenue between Moraga and Noriega Streets, on Noriega between 37th and 38th Avenues, and on 29th and 30th Avenues between Ortega and Rivera Streets. McKeon became well known during the "freeway revolt" of the late 1950s, when he vehemently opposed plans to build freeways in San Francisco, including ones through the Sunset and Golden Gate Park (see page 96).

In 1959 the local Eagles group gave McKeon a plaque for his "unselfish devotion to the City of San Francisco." Mayor George Christopher named him chair of the Mayor's Committee on Freeways, and he was later named a director of the Golden Gate Bridge and Highway District. He died on August 29, 1967.

FERNANDO NELSON

Fernando Nelson was born in New York City on February 4, 1860. He moved to San Francisco when he was fifteen years old and began building houses when he was twenty-two.

Fernando Nelson & Sons are best known for building houses in San Francisco's Eureka Valley, Noe Valley, Richmond, and West Portal neighborhoods. In 1916 the company started building what are perhaps the grandest homes in the Sunset District. Parkway Terrace was a "restricted" development (see chapter 9) from Lincoln Way to Irving Street between 27th Avenue and 33rd Avenue. A 1916 newspaper article touted the new home Nelson had built for himself at 2701 Lincoln Way at 28th Avenue. However, after building the first two blocks of houses from 27th to 28th Avenue, Nelson & Sons sold the rest of the blocks of Parkway Terrace to finance the company's development in West Portal.

Fernando Nelson died in 1953 at the age of ninety-three.

Fernando Nelson & Sons built these concrete benches on Lincoln Way before building the houses in Parkway Terrace. Note the ungraded sand dunes in the background.

This image of the house Fernando Nelson built for himself and his family appeared in the *San Francisco Chronicle* on February 12, 1916.

PROMINENT PROLIFIC BUILDERS

RAY (R. F.) GALLI (CA. 1892–1969)

With an office at 377 West Portal Avenue, Galli Construction Company built a large number of houses in San Francisco's Sunset, Merced Manor, Diamond Heights, and Silver Avenue neighborhoods. The company slogan, found on billboards and in advertising, proclaimed, "Galli-Built Means Better Built" (sometimes "Galli-Built Means Better Bilt").

R. F. Galli opened a number of model homes to promote his developments, including

Ray (R. F.) Galli

- The Carmel, 1554 39th Avenue (1939)
- Casa Moderna, 1590 39th Avenue (1940) (no longer standing)
- Century House, 2819 Rivera Street (1951)
- Challenger, 2278 44th Avenue (1942)
- Holiday House, 2163 44th Avenue (1942)
- The Parkway ("An American Beauty Model Home"), 2627 37th Avenue (1940)
- Priority House, 2191 44th Avenue (1941)
- The Rivera, 2191 45th Avenue (1941)
- Spring Haven, 2614 38th Avenue
- The Thrift Home, 3324 Moraga Street (1940)
- The Vicente, 2621 Vicente Street (1941)

The R. F. Galli sales office was at 377 West Portal Avenue. The building still stands.

One of Galli's houses in the Sunset.

The Parkway House model home on 37th Avenue.

"Galli houses were built by union labor. Dad said that he didn't believe in working the guys by lantern light. Dad wanted the guys to be home with their families by 4:30 or 5 o'clock. And if they were earning a living wage, they could go buy the same house for themselves. That was his philosophy at the time."

—

Ron Galli

"My dad told me that one day a woman came by and said, 'Why do we have to walk up the front stairs of these houses and walk through one room to another room?' That gave him an idea. He stayed up all night to do some drawings on his own. The next day, he showed these drawings to his architect, Edmund Denke. That's where the tunnel entrance in San Francisco originated. In fact, it was known immediately as 'The Galli Plan' by the FHA. The plan shortened the homes and reduced building costs and the selling price."

—

Ray Galli Jr.

Like many Sunset builders, R. F. Galli built a home for his family in the neighborhood. When he built a row of houses on 28th Avenue, he saved 1574 28th for his family. His wife and two sons, Ray Jr. and Ron, lived there from 1932 to 1940, when they moved to 3090 23rd Avenue.

R. F. Galli and his family lived at 1574 28th Avenue from 1932 to 1940.

R. F. Galli is credited with inventing the common "tunnel entrance,"[4] although since all the builders borrowed from one another, the actual origin of this design can't be determined. To enter this kind of house, a person

One of R. F. Galli's designers may have invented the "tunnel entrance," used by many Sunset District builders. Most tunnel entrances are now covered by security gates.

walks through an entrance at street level, then through a covered concrete patio and up a staircase that leads to the front door, which opens into the center of the house. (In floor plans without the tunnel entrance, the front door opens to a small entryway outside the living and dining rooms.) Introduced in the mid-1930s, the tunnel entrance soon became a popular Sunset house feature used by all builders. It actually "shortened" a house so that it fit better on the 25-by-120-foot lots in the Sunset and cost less to build and buy.

During World War II, when lumber and other materials were hard to get, Galli worked on small, one-story houses on 45th Avenue designed for people who worked in local defense plants. He built approximately fifty of these "defense houses" on 45th Avenue between Quintara and Santiago. He dubbed them "Holiday Houses" and promoted them in ads that read, "Here's a 'Thanks, Uncle Sam' Holiday House."

According to Ray Galli Jr., his father and uncle traveled to Los Angeles, where they saw new "patio homes" being built. Returning to San Francisco, Galli asked his house designer, Edmund Denke, to design similar cottages on 48th Avenue. He named the development Little Hollywood. It featured small cottages that were significantly different from the typical two-story Sunset house.

Ray Galli Jr., spent four years in the Air Force and then joined his father in the building business in the mid-1950s. "I'll never forget it," he said. "My dad told me to supervise some apartments we were building on Taraval Street. I didn't know a stud from a cripple, and I learned a lot in that six or eight months building those buildings!" His brother, Ron, later joined the firm, which was then building outside the city in Pleasanton, Marin County, and Hillsborough.

"My dad almost fainted at one of the model homes when one of the salesmen saw this beautiful bush and cut it and put it as a display in the dining room. The beautiful bush was poison oak!"

—

Ray Galli Jr.

"I remember going through a tunnel entrance and climbing those stairs to visit a lovely young girl who most likely was a fellow student from Lincoln High, all the while hoping her parents weren't there, so we could dance on her living room carpet in our stocking feet. I can still hear the sound of those big bands playing romantic ballads as we both moved effortlessly to that mellow beat."

—

Steve Aguado

"The lots in the Sunset all looked the same. You'd go out there and it would be all sand. One time, Henry Doelger started a house on one of my dad's lots. Dad's superintendent, Andy, came in one day and said, 'Hey, there's a house on one of your lots!' My dad called up Doelger. Nowadays, there would be a lawsuit and court hearings. Instead, my dad and Doelger switched lots and made a deal. They were all a pretty good group of builders."

—

Ray Galli Jr.

In the early 1960s Galli Construction Company built three- and four-bedroom units in the Diamond Heights redevelopment project. "This is the first time in our thirty-eight years of building that we used architects," the company announced. Ray Galli's sons, Ron and Ray Jr., continue the Galli legacy through their company, Galli Heritage, which still operates in Burlingame, a suburb south of San Francisco.

Galli designed this row of "Holiday Houses" on 45th Avenue for World War II defense workers.

These "Little Hollywood" houses on 48th Avenue—not to be confused with the Little Hollywood neighborhood in another part of San Francisco—were similar to cottages that R. F. Galli had seen in southern California.

A row of Galli homes in the Sunset.

CARL GELLERT (1898–1974) AND
FRED GELLERT (1901–1978)

The Gellert brothers, Carl and Fred, founded Standard Building Company, which built its first house in the central Sunset in 1922. In those early days, fighting the sand dunes was a constant battle. According to a company history, "One early effort at advertising was thwarted when a high wind filled the street in front of a model home at 31st Avenue and Santiago with so much sand that potential buyers couldn't reach the house."[5]

Carl Gellert

Standard Building Company had company offices in various locations. The best-known office was built in 1948 at 2222 19th Avenue. Other buildings included a warehouse at 23rd and Vicente, a main office at 1500 Judah Street, a garage for heavy equipment on Vicente near 36th Avenue, and a mill on Sloat Boulevard where the Gellerts later built the Lakeshore Shopping Center.

Fred Gellert

Standard Building Company built extensively in the Sunset in the 1940s and marketed the houses as Sunstream Homes, a name the company trademarked. A plaque in the basement of each house informed people that they were standing in a Sunstream Home.

Standard Building Company model homes in the 1940s included

- The Sunstream 1940 on 31st Avenue near Quintara

- The Sunstream Del Mar at 42nd Avenue and Judah Street

- The Sunstream Vicente at 2543 45th Avenue

- The Sunstream Octagon at 2740 35th Avenue

Carl and Fred Gellert put plaques in the basements of many of their Sunstream Homes.

"I got married in 1944, and we moved to this house built by Standard Building Company. One of my first memories of the sounds in the Sunset was every day, constantly all day long, hammer hammer hammer, pound pound pound. And the saws. They would cut the wood out there. You'd hear that saw going and the pounding. All day long, year after year, developing the Sunset."

—

Frances Larkin

"We bought our first house from Standard Building Company in 1947. We saw a model on 43rd Avenue, and we could tell them what colors we wanted. Ours was the fifth from the corner of Wawona Street. All the houses looked the same. The only way we could tell ours was to count in from the corner. Once the blue trim we had chosen was painted on the outside, we knew which house was ours."

—

Edythe Newman

"Standard Building Company created more than forty companies for building, sales, advertising, land investment, and more. Each one had a different name, including Bay Area Contractors, Trelleg (Gellert backward) Construction Co., and Salta (Atlas backward). At one time, Standard Building Company was challenged by the IRS, and the case took three to four years. Eventually, 75 percent of the companies were allowed. Those disallowed were merged into the other companies."

—

Peter Brusati

The Gellerts also produced a document, "Instructions for the Care and Maintenance of Sunstream Homes," which they also hung in the houses. This document gave advice, saying, "We advise everyone who purchases one of our 'SUNSTREAM HOMES' to read these instructions carefully and by practicing them continually you will get the most satisfactory service and greatest enjoyment from your 'SUNSTREAM HOME.'" Advice included, "Do not over heat home when new. Over heating will cause excessive shrinkage and materially damage your home. ... Do not nail radio poles, etc., on your roof. ... Always keep the bathroom window open about 1-1/2 inches on top. ... Do not slam doors. ... Do not slam the door on the mirror medicine cabinet. ... When pulling up window shades do not let them roll up on their own accord. ... Be sure to add cold water in all plumbing fixtures before adding hot water. ... Keep small keys for bath and bedroom doors in a convenient place in case they are accidentally locked from inside. ... Do not use water or gasoline on hardwood floors. ... Drain all the water from the water heater once a month. ... Water your lawn every day."

A prominent Standard Building Company office at 2222 19th Avenue. The building still stands.

An ad in the *San Francisco Chronicle* for the Sunstream Octagon offered:

8 Reasons Why!

1. This home IS completely different

2. More economical—In cost and upkeep

3. Compact—but has more living area

4. Has larger rooms—more skillfully arranged

5. Is the last word in convenience

6. Definitely more livable

7. Allows more sunlight and air

8. Most astounding home value ever offered[6]

Standard Building Company built the Sunstream Octagon model home at 2740 35th Avenue in 1940. The "Octagon" was not an eight-sided house. The name referred to the "8 reasons why" (see at right).

Sales boomed. The *San Francisco Chronicle* reported on July 21, 1940, that sales of Sunstream homes during the first three weeks of July that year were double the number for the entire month of July the previous year. Building slowed during World War II, but in the late 1940s, Sunstream homes were being built in San Francisco and South San Francisco at the rate of three per day.

Peter Brusati, who worked at Standard Building Company for forty years, said, "The Gellerts really took care of their employees. At the holiday party in December, each employee received an envelope with a minimum of two weeks' pay, unless the employee was new. Some received one month's pay or more."[7] In 1958 Brusati helped set up the Carl and Celia B. Gellert Foundation.

During World War II, the Gellerts built military installations and housing at bases in Oakland, Pittsburg, Stockton, Richmond, and Treasure Island. After the war, they built Lakeshore Plaza Shopping Center on Sloat Boulevard and the Forest Knolls development. Later, they moved their business south to Daly City and South San Francisco. Their largest project was in Serramonte (Daly City) and included the shopping center, 2,000 homes, and 500 apartments.

The Gellerts also built in Ardenwood, Country Club Acres (east of the San Francisco Zoo), Forest Hill, Lake Merced, Lakeside, Mount Sutro, and Twin Peaks. In 1941 Carl Gellert was elected secretary of the National Association of Home Builders. He was later quoted as saying, "We can stand on any hill in San Francisco and look down on some home or apartment we have built." [8]

OLIVER M. ROUSSEAU (1891–1977)

Oliver Rousseau

"My father was the youngest of seven children. He was a trained architect, not a 'developer.' His Sunset work was at the beginning of his career. Later, he built houses and apartments in neighborhoods east of the Sunset District and outside San Francisco."

—

Rosemarie (Rousseau) Wagner, daughter of Oliver Rousseau

"You can hardly believe the snobbery of the people in those houses built by Rousseau. I was at a bridge party across the street [on 34th Avenue], and I was sick and tired of hearing those neighbors saying that their houses had steel girders [I-beams] under them. And they do! I finally said, 'You know, putting steel girders under a five-room house is like putting concrete pillars under a birdcage.' I didn't get more popular for saying that, but it was the truth. Rousseau built elaborate, beautiful houses with step-down living rooms, gates between the dining and living rooms, and other crazy things— too elaborate for my taste."

—

Marie McCormack (born 1907)

"Our Rousseau house on 34th Avenue was built in 1934. My husband and I picked this house as it was being built. Rousseau was known for including sunken living rooms and other extras. My mother warned us: 'Buy without a sunken living room so people won't trip and fall.' We paid $6,700 for the house, a lot of money then."

—

Marcella Ames

Most Sunset house builders were not trained architects. An exception was Oliver M. Rousseau, a licensed architect.[9] He apprenticed under his father, Charles Rousseau, who was born in Holland and studied architecture at École des Beaux-Arts in Paris. Oliver got his start in the Sunset District, where, in the early 1930s, he built houses that were grander and more whimsical than the typical neighborhood houses. His houses are grouped primarily in the 1500 blocks between 34th and 41st Avenues; some also appear in West Portal, Pacific Heights, and the Marina.

On the outside, Rousseau houses look castle-like with turrets, balconies, towers, and weather vanes. Inside, the houses feature sunken living rooms, hand-painted designs on ceiling beams and walls, and metal gates separating the living and dining rooms. In 1932, Oliver Rousseau built a house for his family at 1598 36th Avenue, later the home of Audley and Josephine Cole (see chapter 9).

Rousseau used "fancier" designs when building his houses, which always cost a little more than the houses by Henry Doelger, R. F. Galli, and other Sunset District builders.

During World War II, Rousseau built houses for war workers in Richmond, San Bruno, Vallejo, Benicia, Watsonville, Oakland, and other cities. After the war, he built houses outside of San Francisco, in Richmond, Hayward, and Sacramento, often under the business name TORO (The Oliver Rousseau Organization). Oliver and his brother, Arthur, went on to form the Rousseau Brothers and became known for building fine houses and duplexes in other San Francisco neighborhoods and later in Richmond, Hayward, and Sacramento.

Oliver later served on San Francisco's Planning Commission and Public Utilities Commission. He died on May 30, 1977, at the age of eighty-six.

From 1933 to 1935, Oliver Rousseau and his family lived in this house he built at 1598 36th Avenue.

HENRY DOELGER: THE MOST PROLIFIC BUILDER

Henry Doelger

The builder of the greatest number of houses in the Sunset was Henry Doelger. He built thousands of homes in the 1930s and 1940s, replacing the sand dunes with row after row of similar-looking houses. While many builders erected houses on the Sunset sand dunes, none approached the prolific building of Henry Doelger.

Estimates of the number of houses Doelger built vary, but people agree that he built thousands. According to an article in the newsletter published by San Francisco Architectural Heritage, Doelger built 2,800 homes in the Sunset. He repeatedly claimed in his advertisements that he was America's biggest homebuilder between 1934 and 1940. He has been referred to as the largest homebuilder in the country until William Levitt built Levittown on Long Island, New York, after World War II. Most estimates say that at one point Doelger was completing two houses a day in the Sunset.

Henry Doelger was born in San Francisco in 1896. His family lived at Mason Street and Pacific Avenue. When Henry was eight years old, his father, John, opened a grocery store, John Doelger Liquors, at 7th Avenue and Hugo Street in the Inner Sunset. John and his wife, Julia, lived upstairs at 543 Hugo with their three sons: Frank, Henry, and John.

Henry attended St. Ignatius School on Hayes and Shrader Streets for several years. His connection to St. Ignatius was renewed in 1965 when the school hired him as special adviser, "responsible for the planning and construction phases" of the new school building.[10]

When Henry was twelve years old, his father died. Henry dropped out of school and helped his older brother, Frank, run a saloon next to the grocery store, at 1250 7th Avenue. This saloon was the object of a "holdup spree" in late 1915: according to author Kevin Mullen, four men "held up a saloon run by Henry Doelger at 7th Avenue and Hugo Street."[11]

Not just a saloon owner, Frank Doelger had a real estate office at 743 Irving Street. He began teaching Henry what he knew about the business.

People often ask where Henry Doelger got the money to become such a prolific builder. He always said he earned money by running a hot dog stand in his childhood. A grandniece has given a different account: "My grandfather told us the story many times of brewing bathtub gin and homemade beer to sell at a tamale stand they had in Golden Gate Park. Henry invested all the earnings from the stand in land purchased from artichoke farmers, which he was told he was crazy for trying to build on since it was mostly sand."[12]

In 1922, Henry Doelger bought land at 14th Avenue and Irving for $1,100. Soon he learned that a movie house, the second Irving Theatre, would be built close by. "Prices went wild when the rumor started about a theater on Irving," according to his son Michael.[13]   A few months later, Henry reportedly sold the land at a great profit.

In the 1920s, Henry Doelger bought his first large piece of property: the block (#1814) bounded by 39th Avenue, Judah Street, 40th

The first Henry Doelger house, built in 1927, stands at 1427 39th Avenue.

Avenue, and Kirkham Street.[14]   Henry built twenty-five homes on the 39th Avenue side of this block.

When Frank died unexpectedly in 1932, Henry formed his own company and hired his younger brother, John. According to Ed

"Across the street from our house, in the residential area [at Hugo Street and 7th Avenue], was Mr. Doelger's saloon. The family, consisting of Frank, John, and Henry, lived above it. … One night, I was awakened by the sound of gunshots outside my bedroom window. The next day I found out there had been a hold-up at Mr. Doelger's saloon … the shots had been fired at the fleeing robbers."

—

Hazel Drescher Schaffer (born 1907), "Hazel's Memoirs: Growing Up in San Francisco"

"My father's older brother, Frank, taught him how to buy and sell lots, how to speculate. My father bought lots, but during the hard economic times there were no buyers for 'raw lots.' My father had over-extended himself by buying these lots and had to recoup his costs. He hooked up with Carl Vedell. They hired a few carpenters and built a few houses. When these sold, they built more. His success in building and selling grew out of necessity: he couldn't sell empty lots, but with houses on them he could."

—

Michael Doelger

"In those days, most of the Sunset was sand dunes. It wasn't like it is now. I remember you could get a lot for $300—$300 for a sand lot. And then we had this Henry Doelger. He came out and started to build houses, and then it got developed and developed."

—

Jack Goldsworthy

"My father admired the assembly-line ideas of Henry Ford. On his jobs, Doelger broke crews down into areas of specialization, and they worked only in those areas: foundations, framing, and carpentry."

—

Michael Doelger,
son of Henry and Thelma Doelger

"My three brothers and I owned a furniture store, the Associated Home Furnishers. We were fortunate to get the contract for all the window shades in the Doelger homes. Later we got the contract for Venetian blinds. We had that contract for many years, so about 90 percent of shades and blinds in Doelger homes were supplied by our store."

—

Stan Adair

"Doelger's first office was in the back of a garage near the corner of 8th and Judah. The Doelgers owned the apartment house. He took a space in the garage of that apartment house, and that was his office, until they built the offices at 320 Judah."

—

Ed Hageman,
former draftsman for Henry Doelger

"My father didn't like Henry Doelger because my father designed houses in the Sunset and then Doelger came in and became famous. My father felt that Doelger got all the credit for developing the Sunset when there were others."

—

Rosemarie (Rousseau) Wagner,
daughter of Oliver Rousseau

Hageman, who worked for Henry Doelger when he was building in the Sunset, John Doelger was the "overall superintendent" and Henry's "right-hand man."

Over time, Henry Doelger bought fourteen undeveloped blocks in the Sunset at $10,000 each. Once he had built and sold a few homes, he had the seed money to build more. However, his extensive building still required a sizable bank loan. According to Michael Doelger, "My father took A. P. Giannini [president of Bank of America] for a ride out to the Sunset to show him what he was doing." As a result, Giannini told the people at the bank to give Henry Doelger "everything he needed." Doelger started with $110,000 from Bank of America in 1936 and eventually received close to $75 million in loans from that bank.[15]

Doelger said that his Sunset houses were "the outgrowth of a boyhood dream that one day the desolate sand dunes of the Sunset might be replaced by trim modern homes, owned by 'Mr. and Mrs. Average San Franciscan,'" and that he (Henry Doelger) "would have a part in this vast undertaking."[16]

When people think of the houses in the Sunset District, they often refer to the "Doelger style," with a garage on the ground floor and living quarters upstairs. While Doelger did not invent this style of house (for example, look at the houses built in 1929 in the 1400 block of York Street in the Mission District), he and others used it because the lots in the Sunset were small—25 by 120 feet. Garages on the street level could accommodate cars, and there was plenty of living space above. While many families did not have automobiles in the 1930s, cars were clearly seen as part of the future; by the 1920s, many new houses and apartment buildings had garages.

The floor plans of most Doelger houses in the central Sunset were the same. The "elevations," or fronts of homes, differed. Some featured wooden or metal balconies; others had faux window shutters; others were covered by different types of roofs. After his draftsmen generated ideas for the elevations, Henry and John Doelger strung wires across one side and across the other side of his conference room, representing two Sunset blocks facing each other. The elevations were repeated, but the Doelgers carefully chose the designs for each block so that the repetition was not noticeable.

Henry Doelger planned and sold his houses from his office at 320 Judah Street. A strong marketer, his name appeared three times on the outside of the building. The building still stands and is being considered for landmark status by the City and County of San Francisco.

Henry Doelger houses can be found throughout the Sunset, but his major developments were in the area he called "Doelger City," 26th to 36th Avenue between Kirkham and Quintara Streets.[17] People often disparaged his houses because they looked so similar and seemed featureless. Some people had names for Henry Doelger as well. One was "one-nail Doelger." The origin of this name is not clear. Some people say it referred to shoddy construction; others say that when Henry Doelger was asked how he built so many houses, he replied, "One nail at a time."

The Art Deco building at 320 Judah was designed by Charles O. Clausen, a Doelger architect, and housed Doelger's sales and work offices during his years of greatest production in the Sunset, from 1932 to the early 1950s.

In the 1930s people bought houses built by Doelger for about $5,000, a large amount of money during the Great Depression. "During the Depression," said Michael Doelger, "my father held second mortgages on many of the homes he built in the Sunset. He didn't 'forgive' the loans indefinitely, but in those days there were often balloon payments that people couldn't make. He would ask, 'Can you pay anything?' If not, he would renegotiate the note and wait for the house buyer's financial situation to improve."

Ed Hageman met Doelger as a child and later worked for him, designing houses in the Sunset and in the Westlake area of Daly City, south of San Francisco. "I was about twelve years old when my mother and father bought what I think was the thirty-fifth home that Doelger built," said Hageman. "It was on 39th Avenue between Judah and Kirkham. Henry Doelger came to our home on Fillmore and talked to my mother and dad. He had a few notes with him—nothing sophisticated

"Henry Doelger was nice to people who were nice to him. He was a friend of my father's, and they ran across each other all the time. Once Doelger was building in the block above us, between 12th and 13th [now Funston] Avenues. Doelger asked my father, 'Do you need anything?' We needed wood for our fireplace. 'What size do you want?' Then Doelger turned to one of his workers and said, 'Give this man anything he asks for.'"

—

Catherine Murphy (born 1914)

"Doelger knew that he would have to build houses that would sell quickly. He shrewdly realized that the greatest market lay in the masses of families who wanted homes of their own but could not afford the normal price of a separate house. His solution was a row house of a kind never before built on such a scale."

—

Harold Gilliam,
The Face of San Francisco, p. 88

like a portfolio or anything like that. He was just building houses and selling them."[18]

When Hageman was around twenty years old, he began working for Henry Doelger. "I started as a draftsman," Hageman said. Later, he worked for John Doelger on building sites. "I used to see that the houses were finished properly. It was my job to select the colors for the bathrooms and the kitchens and keep the subcontractors on target so that they'd get in and finish up their portions of the houses. We had many subcontractors—plumbers, electricians, bricklayers, tile setters, and so on."

Hageman and Henry Doelger got along well. "He always liked me and was always good to me. When my wife and I were married, he gave us the down payment on our home as a wedding present."

Henry Doelger was a consummate marketer who knew how to promote his name and his houses. Like the Gellerts, whenever Doelger built a house, he hung a metal plaque in the basement with the number of the house. "It kept the Doelger name in front of everyone," said Michael Doelger.

Ed Hageman (center rear) in 1930, surrounded by his pals and the new Doelger homes on 39th Avenue. Hageman, who as a child lived in a Doelger home on 39th Avenue, later became Doelger's top designer.

Doelger also sponsored contests to bring prospective customers to his model homes. The contests were popular ways for people to learn about (and maybe purchase) new Doelger homes. For example, in the "Name Please" contest, held in late 1940, Doelger invited people to rename the model home at 1754 19th Avenue, originally called Normandy. The first-place winner chose from $100 in cash, a General Electric refrigerator, or an Occidental gas range. After 12,000 entries, a new name was given to the home style: the Doelworth.

In a 1942 contest, Doelger asked the public to complete the statement, "I am glad I am an American because …" The prizes included U.S. defense bonds and a $75 gift certificate for Redlick's, the store that had furnished the home. In order to enter the contest, people had to visit a new Doelger model home, the Freedom House, at 1738 43rd Avenue. Newspaper articles about the contest and the Freedom House ("designed and furnished with an emphasis on the economy required by the Nation's war program") ran side by side with Doelger ads ("priced unbelievably low: yet it sparkles with a score of 'extras' which make every DOELGER HOME a far better value").

Thousands of contest entries poured in. The awards were later distributed, not at the Freedom House

Henry Doelger invited the public to a model home ("Normandy") at 1754 19th Avenue to pick up an entry form for the "Name Please" contest.

To enter Henry Doelger's "Defense Bond Contest," people had to pick up entry forms at the Freedom House model home at 1738 43rd Avenue.

model but at the Nantucket, a new model home at 1851 33rd Avenue. The winner was Richmond District resident Edward O'Brien, who had written, "I am glad I am an American because my life is my own to live and enjoy; my country a pleasure to defend."

Other model homes were promoted to the public through Doelger ads and through real estate "articles" in the newspaper. For example, in May 1938 a local newspaper wrote, "More than 4,000 people visited the Trianon. … Its features include a sky room den, streamlined bath, club car breakfast nook and mirrored fireplace."

Other Doelger model homes included

- The Lexington in Golden Gate Heights (January 1940)

- The Forty-Finer (probably a reference to the year the house was built) at 1538 40th Avenue (March 1940)

- El Dorado at 1614 41st Avenue (June 1940)

- The Lafayette at 1750 34th Avenue (1941)

- The American at 1958 30th Avenue (1941)

- The Styleocrat at 3430 Moraga Street (1941)

- The Courtland at 1746 35th Avenue (1941)

The winner of the "Defense Bond Contest" was announced at a new Doelger home model, the Nantucket, on 33rd Avenue.

The Georgian at 1739 33rd Avenue (July 1940) and the Oceanica at 1751 33rd Avenue (September 1940) shared a floor plan that was different from most Doelger homes: the living and dining rooms were at the rear of the house, instead of at the front. These houses were on the west side of the street, and Doelger knew how to use an ocean view in his marketing. One ad said, "We've called it 'The Oceanica' because of the marvelous, sweeping view it commands of the sparkling Pacific."

Most Doelger houses in the central Sunset District were small (two bedrooms, one bathroom), but he also built grander houses in Golden Gate Heights. In the 1930s, before he became famous for building houses, Henry Doelger purchased a two-block stretch of land on 15th Avenue from Carl Larsen (see chapter 9). Author William Saroyan commissioned a home for his mother and sister on 15th Avenue, near Noriega. Built on the side of the hill, this three-story house featured bedrooms upstairs; a garage, living room, and kitchen on the ground floor; and a downstairs level with a bathroom, bedroom, and workroom for Saroyan himself. Saroyan studied and wrote in this room, which had a sweeping view of the Sunset neighborhood and the Pacific Ocean.

Doelger built a large house at 1995 15th Avenue, where he and his family lived from 1938 to the early 1950s. On the same block of 15th Avenue he built several homes that are larger than those he built elsewhere in the Sunset. Each house had an outside mailbox that was a miniature replica of the house. (Most of these mailboxes are gone now.) According to Michael Doelger, Henry had driven around Beverly Hills looking at the large homes. The houses he built on this block were scaled-down versions of what he had seen in southern California.

Henry Doelger built his own home at 1995 15th Avenue, where his family lived from 1938 until the early 1950s.

This house, built for author William Saroyan, stands on 15th Avenue in Golden Gate Heights.

Is this a Doelger home? Yes! He built a block of homes on 15th Avenue in Golden Gate Heights in the 1930s. Inspired by the grand houses he had seen in southern California, each house had a mailbox that matched the house. This house still has its original mailbox (see enlargement, upper left).

"I worked at Arrow Shirt Co. in Apparel City. Henry Doelger used to come in with his entourage and buy shirts by the box at wholesale prices. He had a luncheon every Wednesday at the Westlake Golf Course for friends and business associates. I had a standing invitation as long as I continued to sell him shirts. I went once. There was a long table with politicians and builders."

—

Bill Kleeman

"Henry Doelger was a yachtsman. He didn't give a damn what people thought about him. He'd be out yachting all day and come in without a shave, in dirty clothes that smelled like fish. He'd walk into the best clubs in the city with his yachting clothes on, but no one ever questioned him because he had so much money. Mr. Doelger was a big person. And he was actually a pretty nice person."

—

Fred Van Dyke

"My husband built wood moldings for Henry Doelger when he was building large houses on two blocks of 15th Avenue. My father-in-law, Fred Warden [one of the smaller Sunset builders], knew Henry Doelger when he was selling bootleg liquor in the early 1920s. Fred built apartment houses in the Sunset. The Thelma Apartments on 8th Avenue were named after Doelger's wife."

—

Jeanne Warden

By the end of the 1940s, Doelger had finished his work in the Sunset. He had bought 1,350 acres in Daly City from Spring Valley Water Company in 1945, and in the early 1950s he moved his office to South Mayfair Avenue in Daly City. He built houses in Westlake and other parts of Daly City until 1962. He built his own home there, at 112 Northgate Avenue, and spent the rest of his life as a resident of Daly City.

Malvina Reynolds wrote a song in 1962, criticizing a row of Henry Doelger houses that had appeared on a hillside above Skyline Boulevard in Daly City. The chorus said:

> Little boxes on the hillside,
> Little boxes made of ticky tacky,
> Little boxes on the hillside,
> Little boxes all the same.
> There's a green one and a pink one
> And a blue one and a yellow one,
> And they're all made out of ticky tacky
> And they all look just the same.*

While the song refers to new Doelger-built houses, it also reflected the general view that all Sunset District houses looked alike and lacked the variety and details of the Victorian and Edwardian buildings of "old San Francisco." Others pointed out, however, that while the Sunset and Daly City houses might lack the graceful details found in older buildings, these new houses gave moderate-income families the opportunity to own their own homes in new developments.

Henry Doelger died of a heart attack at age eighty-two on July 23, 1978.

The Developed Neighborhood

By the mid-1900s, most of the Sunset District's sand dunes were covered with houses and streets. The early complications caused by shifting sands were mostly gone. After World War II, a flood of families moved to the Sunset, increasing the population and bringing a second wave of pioneers to the neighborhood.

The last large sand dune in the Sunset was covered in 1969 when St. Ignatius College Preparatory, a Catholic high school formerly on Stanyan Street, built a new campus on 37th Avenue.

"Maybe the last guy who really provided affordable housing was an unlikely fellow named Henry Doelger who covered the sands of the Sunset with row upon row of houses—hundreds of them, selling at about $5000 each, an excellent value to this day. Henry Doelger was a fun-loving, playboy-ish kind of man who, in one incredible stretch in the 1940s, built a house a day. He built so many, in fact, that he lost one 'and I never found it,' he once chuckled. Somebody in the Sunset may be living in a free house that nobody knows about."

—

Herb Caen, columnist,
San Francisco Sunday Examiner and Chronicle, July 7, 1985

"My uncle used to furnish houses for Henry Doelger. In 1974, Mr. Doelger brought two dozen red roses to my grandmother for her ninetieth birthday. As he sat with us, he waved his hand toward the Sunset District and said, 'I can't believe I created this whole thing.'"

—

Sandy Baumgarten

Doelger's rows of new houses in Daly City, seen here from the entrance to the Mission Drive-in Theater, inspired Malvina Reynolds's song, "Little Boxes."

Notes

1. Interview with R. F. Galli's sons, Ron Galli and Ray Galli Jr., March 5, 2005.

2. *San Francisco Chronicle,* April 4, 1931.

3. James McDonagh's biographical information was provided by his son, Steve McDonagh.

4. Interview with Ron Galli and Ray Galli Jr., March 5, 2005.

5. *Sunstream Homes: 50 Golden Years of Home Building Excellence,* p. 6.

6. *San Francisco Chronicle,* September 1, 1940.

7. Interview with Peter Brusati, October 17, 2004.

8. Stephanie Salter, "Home-building Brothers Change the Map of San Francisco," *San Francisco Examiner,* March 11, 1985.

9. Interview with Rosemarie Rousseau Wagner, February 12, 2004.

10. Paul Totah, *Spiritus "Magis": 150 Years of Saint Ignatius College Preparatory,* p. 130.

11. Kevin Mullen, *The Toughest Gang in Town,* pp. 224–28.

12. Leslie LaManna, granddaughter of John Doelger, as quoted on the Western Neighborhoods Project website (http://www.outsidelands.org/sw2.php).

13. All comments by Michael Doelger (Henry Doelger's son) are from an interview conducted February 9, 2004.

14. San Francisco Block Book, 1920.

15. Marquis James and Bessie Rowland James, *A Biography of a Bank: The Story of Bank of America,* p. 490.

16. Pamphlet: *America's Fastest Selling Homes Are Built by Doelger.*

17. Ibid.

18. Interview with Ed Hageman, October 21, 2006.

When St. Ignatius High School announced plans to move to the Sunset, this photo appeared on the cover of the *Genesis* newsletter with the caption, "It appears that the first class at the sixth campus of S.I. has been scheduled a bit prematurely."

Constructing buildings in the Parkside sand dunes.

CHAPTER 6

PIONEERS INHABIT THE DUNES, 1930s–1950s

The Sunset was a developed neighborhood by the time this photo was taken in 1944.

Many people who lived in the Sunset in the 1930s and 1940s were "pioneers," residents in a new neighborhood that seemed to spring up overnight. Here were families who owned their homes for the first time, instead of renting flats in other city neighborhoods. They lived through the transition from sand dunes to blocks of housing and busy streets and created a new community far from the older, more crowded areas of San Francisco.

Many of these pioneering residents could hear lions roar at Fleishhacker Zoo, even though their homes were more than a mile away. One woman complained in a local newspaper about being unable to plant a garden in her sand-blown backyard. Some people recollect "sandstorms" that made the roads impassable and destroyed automobiles parked on the street.

This chapter captures residents' memories of the growing neighborhood from the 1930s through the 1950s.

WEATHER AND DUNES

Most older and former Sunset residents talk about the weather and the sand. Rain and fog—and eternal grayness—seem to permeate most people's memories. The rain seemed heavier and the fog seemed ever-present. The weather might have been more severe than it is now, or the perceived

"I remember living on 43rd Avenue. The Great Highway from Noriega to Rivera would fill with water after winter storms. It was like a pond, and people could row up the water in boats. My dad told me that when he was courting my mother in the teens or twenties, he would row from his house to hers."

—

Alex Spotorno

"In the thirties, windstorms caused people to be sanded in much the way people in other climates are snowed in. It was an adventure for the kids but a royal pain for my mother and father. When the wind blew, it penetrated everything. The garage would fill up with sand, and the car— you'd hope it wouldn't penetrate into the motor. Some people who left their cars out on the street found their motors damaged. And after a sandstorm, people needed bulldozers to clear the streets. Sometimes people had to wait three or four days for the bulldozers to reach their street."

—

Fred Van Dyke

"In the 1930s, I delivered the San Francisco News in the Parkside. My route was 30th and 29th Avenues north of Taraval. There were sandstorms, and sometimes the papers were buried under the sand."

—

Andy Casper

"I was a little kid then, but I remember the great storm of 1936. It scared my parents. The water was washing over the Great Highway and coming into our garage on 48th Avenue. Everything washed into the garage: debris, sand."

—

Fred Van Dyke

"I lived in the Richmond District as a kid in the late 1940s. I would ride my Schwinn cruiser through the park and meet my friend who lived in the Sunset. There was sand everywhere, and it got muddy in the rain. We had mud fights after rainstorms and threw mud like snowballs."

—

Wayne Colyer

"When I was going to college in the 1940s, I worked at night driving a truck. You'd go maybe to 3rd or 5th Avenue, trying to cross over and then you'd run into a dead-end street that hadn't been paved. You'd have to back up and go around. Finally, they made a separate map so people would know where the through streets were."

—

Joe Hurley

In this 1942 newspaper photo, Mrs. R. L. Anderson complains, "We were never able to put in a garden. The back fence has been almost buried in the daily sandstorms."

isolation and large number of sand lots might have made it feel that way.

Not all people complain about their early years in the Sunset. Rosemary Morris's parents bought a house at 16th and Vicente in 1933. Their friends warned them about "moving into the fog." In 1980, looking back at those times, Morris said, "Life in the Sunset wasn't as dismal as predicted. Since everybody was new on the block, it was easy to make friends. The women had bridge parties, the men played poker, and the kids played together in the sand, building castles and digging caves."[1] In fact, children loved the sand dunes, viewing them as part of their nearby playground.

John Keenan remembered a high school prank. He and a friend had practiced walking like a gorilla for a few days and then rented a gorilla suit from a costume shop. "Our adventure started at the zoo on Saturday night," he explained. "We took turns running out of the main entrance at the stoplight in front of cars on Sloat Boulevard. We went over to Lincoln Way, and when cars drove by, we would run out of Golden Gate Park and shinny up a light

"We'd take apart an old barrel and remove the redwood staves. We'd smooth them down and tie them around our feet and ankles. We saw skiing in a movie, and skiing in the sand was our creative way of doing it. The sand dunes were fine for skiing, even though you didn't get much speed. In those days it was probably 100 feet to the bottom of some of the dunes—and they were steep."

—

Fred Van Dyke

"The Sunset District was still being built up during those years. As kids we went out beyond Twentieth Avenue and made believe we were in the French Foreign Legion, charging up and down sand dunes that stretched all the way to the beach."

—

Jerry Flamm,
Good Life in Hard Times, p. 4

The high dunes were great places to climb and play.

pole. We then went to Sunset Boulevard and did the same thing." While they were busy imitating gorillas, the boys did not notice an approaching police car. The policeman asked John if he had been drinking. "I told him no," said John. "I was just out having a good time. He told me to go to another district to have fun. As I left, I noticed that both the cops were laughing."

SWIMMING IN THE SUNSET

Most people think of the Sunset District as a flat and monotonous landscape. However, the land had to be graded to make it even and nearly flat. Early photographs show that some sand dunes were very high and other areas were deeply recessed. At the bottom of at least one of these recessed areas was a small body of water fed by rains or perhaps underground springs. It isn't clear where this body of water lay—or if there were several in the Sunset. Charles Williams remembered the Rivera Street Pond on Rivera between 31st and 32nd Avenues (see photo); Mark Rivero, who swam in a pond in the 1930s, thinks it may have been somewhere else. A newspaper article in 1937 describes "the old water hole at Ortega and 35th Avenue." The boys who swam in it "thought it the loneliest spot in the Parkside District, but the Health Department considered it not too lonely to harbor germs." As the Sunset was graded and developed, these ponds and other waterways disappeared.

Starting in the 1920s, people walked, drove, or took the L Taraval streetcar to Fleishhacker Pool in the Outer Sunset near the zoo. (See chapter 10.)

Children used to swim in this pond at the bottom of the Sunset sand dunes.

"We'd climb up the hills with a flattened cardboard box and then slide down on it."

—

Teresa Hurley

"Some of us used to swim in the swimming hole near Rivera Street. It was in a gully in the sand dunes. The water came from the rains in the wintertime. The water would accumulate at the bottom of this gully, and it was never more than two or three feet deep. You really couldn't swim any distance. They'd close it up every year by putting some tape around it and telling us we'd be arrested if we swam there."

—

Andy Casper

"The boys called it a swimming hole. They didn't have swimming suits, they just went skinny dipping. That swimming hole was contaminated, polluted. When my brother was twelve [circa 1936], he got some kind of germ in his sinus, and it settled in his eye. His eye was protruding out and he almost lost it. They had to do surgery. He had a big scar on his face where they did the surgery. He almost died from it."

—

Frances Larkin

"I used to play a lot in the sand dunes when I was a boy. In fact, my wife—she came from the Sonora area—she said, 'Well, you were born in the city. You didn't know what the country was like.' I said, 'Hell, I saw more country than you, with Golden Gate Park on one side and sand dunes all the way to the beach.'"

—

Ray Galli Jr.

"When we were boys in 1942 or 1943, the dunes beyond Sunset Boulevard were so extensive that we could fantasize that we were in the desert, particularly after we saw films with Humphrey Bogart winning the war in North Africa. This was about seven to ten blocks from 36th and Noriega, down close to the entrance to the zoo on Sloat. It was almost a mile. We'd ride our bikes through the dunes and could lose sight of the houses."

—

William McCormack

"I remember a big sand dune on Taraval at 40th Avenue, on the north side, that went down for about five blocks. It was really huge. You had to walk up quite a hill to get to it. It was still there when I went into the Marine Corps in 1943. It was gone when I returned in 1946."

—

Andy Casper

"My friends and I used to play on the sand hills behind the houses on 15th Avenue. We used to dig large, deep holes and cover them with wood that we 'borrowed' from contractors working in the area, and then cover them with sand and plants. This made great caves for all of us to play in. In later years 14th Avenue was extended from Rivera to Quintara, and the sand hills disappeared."

—

John Keenan, St. Cecilia School
Class of 1960

"Our favorite Saturday afternoon pastime from about 1949 through 1954 was attending the matinee at the Irving Theatre. We would see countless cartoons, a serial, a newsreel, and two features. The admission fee was twenty cents, popcorn was ten cents, ice cream was ten cents, a drink was five cents, and a Sugar Daddy was five cents."

—

Sue Lundblade

"Out on Irving Street around 46th was the Sunset Theatre. That became the Surf. We lived on 45th Avenue, and many times I would take in a movie at the Sunset Theatre. Wallace Beery, Joan Crawford, Robert Taylor—that was the Sunset Theatre."

—

Jack Goldsworthy

"I still remember the first film I saw at the Sunset Theatre. It was High Sierra *starring Humphrey Bogart and Ida Lupino."*

—

Steve Aguado

"The Sunset Theatre? We called it the 'Flea House'!"

—

Dr. Hugh Visser

"As a kid in the 1950s, I remember that we saved up 7-Up bottle caps to get admission to the Parkside Theatre. They also had inexpensive 'kiddie matinees' during the summers, I think on Tuesdays and Thursdays. We'd buy these skinny, perforated tickets at school in early June.

—

Chuck Barnhouse

MOVIE THEATERS

Three movie theaters once thrived in the Sunset: the Irving Theatre on Irving Street near 14th Avenue, the Parkside (renamed the Fox Parkside in 1965) on Taraval Street between 19th and 20th Avenues, and the Parkview (renamed the Sunset in 1937 and then the Surf in 1957) on Irving Street near 46th Avenue. The Sunset Theatre did not have a great reputation, but people today still talk about the Surf Theatre, which was known in the 1950s as an "art house," one of the few public movie houses to show foreign and independent movies. Dorothy Bryant remembers:

> In the 1950s, we could view only formula Hollywood feature films at large movie houses. Then a dinky, dingy old movie house near the beach reopened as the Surf. Waves of viewers from all over San Francisco rolled toward the ocean waves to see the latest at the Surf: archival silents, international films by unknown (later famous) directors, setting a new standard. I learned a lot from seeing these films and from lobby conversations with the interesting people who packed the place. Soon, larger movie houses became aware of this market, and we didn't have to drive all the way to the ocean. But it was the Surf that recognized and fostered

The Parkview Theatre opened in the 1920s. It was renamed the Sunset in 1937 and renamed the Surf in 1957.

The Irving Theatre (shown above in 1941) opened in 1926, closed in 1962 (right), and was torn down in 1963 (below).

the hunger for quality films, rescuing us from the movie palaces featuring the latest star-studded ephemera.

The Irving Theatre opened in 1926. It closed in 1962, was razed the following year, and replaced by an apartment building. The Parkside Theatre opened in 1928 and closed in the 1970s, remade into apartments and a daycare center. The Surf became a church in the 1980s. No movie theaters currently operate in the Sunset.

The Parkside Theater near 19th Avenue was a popular venue for neighborhood residents.

*"I was a young boy, but I remember
when the Boneyard was where
old iron horses retired."*

—

Larry Boysen

*"I spent many an hour wandering
through the Boneyard, marveling at the
wondrous collection of has-been streetcars
and playing motorman at the controls,
most of which could be operated with a
wrench. The imported cars were my
favorites and were all gone by 1941."*

—

Val Golding,
a preteen during the Boneyard years[2]

THE BONEYARD

In the early 1900s the Market Street Railway planned to build a "carbarn," a place where streetcars would be stored and serviced, on a lot between 13th (now Funston) and 14th Avenues, from Lincoln Way to Irving Street. The carbarn was never built, but the railway company began storing obsolete streetcars on this lot, and it soon became known as "the Boneyard." In 1950, the land that housed the Boneyard was sold, and apartments and a grocery store (first Park-and-Shop, now Andronico's) appeared on the land.

HIGH SCHOOL

For many years, the Sunset had no public high school. Most teens who lived in the growing Sunset-Parkside area attended Commerce High School in the Civic Center

The Market Street Railway stored obsolete and deteriorating streetcars on the block bounded by Lincoln Way, Funston Avenue, Irving Street, and 14th Avenue—coincidentally, Cornelius Reynolds's hog farm and house stood in the same spot in the late 1800s (see photograph on page 2). The Boneyard land was sold to developers in 1950.

area or Polytechnic (Poly) High School on Frederick Street, across from Kezar Stadium. In June 1931, Poly High School's yearbook, *The Polytechnic Journal*, printed the following poem by a graduating senior:

"Sand Dunes"

There lies a wild, free stretch of desert land

Between the lashing sea and rugged hills—

The sand dunes brown, that pull back from the hand

Of sea, and swirl into the wind's embracing thrills;

So curving, sun-burned, basking in the sun,

Holding dwarf shrubs that surely live on air,

Feeling the joy of nature's ready fun,

Hearing the bent trees whisper of their care.

A place where I have loved to go and rest

And think of God and skies and sea and land,

And sink close to earth's bosom and be blessed—

A friendly place gone now before the builder's hand.

> *I want the sand dunes to escape the streets;*
>
> *I want to go where nature's heart still beats.*

—Roselle Hansen, '31

When George Washington High School opened in the Richmond District in 1936, many Sunset students transferred to that school.

In 1938, San Francisco voters passed an education bond issue, which provided funds for building Abraham Lincoln High School, still the only public high school ever built in the Sunset District. Located at 2162 24th Avenue, the school sits on four square blocks bounded by 24th Avenue, Quintara Street, 22nd Avenue, and Santiago Street. The four-story building opened in 1940 with fifty classrooms, a cafeteria, a football field (along

"I was in the first class at Lincoln, in the early 1940s. There was no gym—we changed into our physical education (PE) outfits, short blue bloomers, in a classroom. An air raid siren went off during PE, and I had to decide whether to stay at school or go home. I ran in my gym outfit from the school at Quintara to my home at 20th and Kirkham. The door was locked and I had no key, so I ran back to school."

—

Donna Dunn

"I went to Lincoln in the early 1940s. I remember once when the girls wanted to go to school without bobby socks, but the administration wouldn't let them. So all us guys dressed like girls. I wore pedal pushers, and some of the guys wore dresses. It was a great protest before they had protests. They kicked us out, and we'd come back. It lasted a couple of days. I don't think it changed anything; the girls still had to wear bobby socks. But reporters showed up, and the whole city heard about it."

—

Fred Van Dyke

"Originally Lincoln's football field was on Quintara, between 22nd and 23rd or between 23rd and 24th. One year I was on the track team, and the shotputters used to work out right across the street, where the reservoir is now. It was just a sand dune."

—

Andy Casper

Abraham Lincoln High School, when it opened in 1940.

Quintara Street), and a library. The main building could not accommodate all the students, so temporary bungalows with classrooms were placed in the upper yards east of the main school building. (These "temporary" buildings remained in place for sixty years.) According to the school's website, Lincoln's mascot is the mustang because a horse farm used to operate on the land.

In the 1950s, other wings were added to Lincoln, including the Boys' Gym (now called the South Gym), an auditorium, and the Girls' Gym (now called the North Gym). The block just north of Santiago Street was an empty sand-dune lot until the school built a sports stadium on the site in the early 1960s. Gates to the schoolyards were left unlocked, and neighborhood children spent hours in the yards playing kickball, basketball, and hide-and-seek, as well as roller skating, bicycle riding, creating theatrical presentations (on the outside stage), and more. Today, all these gates are kept locked, and new ones on the west side of the school have been constructed to keep all people out, except during school hours.

This 1952 photo shows Parkside District twins Ann Polacchi (now Ann Jennings) and Bob Polacchi, who later attended Lincoln High School. Behind them stands a sand dune at 22nd Avenue and Santiago Street. The school's sports stadium was built on that site around 1960. Also in the background is the Boys' Gym (now called the South Gym) under construction.

A Changing Landscape

The middle of the twentieth century was a period of great development. Areas that had remained impassable because of sand dunes were systematically cut through. Roads and houses were built. And as transportation lines made their way out to the Sunset, more people began buying those houses and moving to the Outside Lands.

In 1938 a local newspaper had recalled the wildness of the area that by that time had changed dramatically: "Little more than a dozen years ago a Hollywood motion picture company shot desert scenes … near 36th Ave. and Ortega-st. and by angling his cameras so that sand dunes hid Golden Gate Park to the north the director created the illusion of a vast desert."[3]

In the early 1940s, Jeanne Warden and her husband moved to the 2100 block of 26th Avenue. At that time, 26th ended at Quintara on the north. Warden remembers that the streets were made of cobblestones, and that when 26th Avenue was cut through, the cobblestones were removed. "The short fence in the back between my building and the building next door is made up of these cobblestones," she says.

Part of the fence in Jeanne Warden's backyard is made of the bricks and cobblestones that were originally part of 26th Avenue.

"I lived on 34th while I was going to Lincoln in the 1940s. There were still dunes, but they were being covered over. I could walk to school all the way through dunes if I wanted to—from 34th Avenue to 24th Avenue. Or I could go up Noriega and up 24th to Lincoln, completely on paved streets."

—

Fred Van Dyke (born 1929)

"When my friend Tim and I were in fourth grade, we played on that quarry where they later built Hoover Junior High. Once I slipped out of Tim's view and was hanging onto a piece of that serpentine rock, scared out of my wits! I started praying, promising every saint that I'd I never climb this rock again. I started shouting for help, and Tim heard me. He walked out onto a ledge, reached down, and pulled me up and out of harm's way. I am sure he saved my life or, at the least, saved me from serious injury. Weeks later, we were both back playing at the quarry."

—

Tom O'Toole, St. Cecilia School, Class of 1960

"We used to love to swing off of the flagpole ropes over at Lincoln High. We also found a secret way to get in there that led to a trap door in the janitor's closet in the girls' locker room. We spent many a weekend roaming around and exploring the high school when it was empty. We tried, but were never successful in getting to the air raid siren on the roof. We really wanted to figure out how to turn it on."

—

Steve Cottrell

"In April of 1932, Mom and Dad made the first major decision in their marriage when they purchased a home at 2570 19th Avenue in San Francisco for $5,000. … Most of the housing at this time ended at 20th Avenue, with sand dunes stretching out to the beach."

—

James L. Mulvany,
Poppy, Our Father: Memories of a Man and His Family, p. 86

"In 1934, when we moved into our home on 34th Avenue, no buildings were in the next block. Doelger later built on that block, but when we moved in, sand would blow onto the lawn from the south. Sometimes an inch of sand covered our lawn!"

—

Marcella Ames

"We moved into our house on 43rd Avenue in 1950. When I cut the lawn on a Saturday, it would take all day because people would come and park, and we'd meet and talk and visit. It was that kind of neighborhood. That's all gone, of course."

—

Joe Hurley

1936: From 15th Avenue and Ortega Street.

When Jeanne Warden's father built their house in 1950, he photographed the progress from empty lot to completed house, as shown below in photos 1, 2, 3, and 4.

1

2

1928: From 12th Avenue and Quintara Street.

1940: The view from Quintara Street has changed a great deal. The arrow points to Abraham Lincoln High School under construction.

3

4

"We spent much of our free time playing outside in the sandlots and in the new construction occurring on our block. As soon as the workers left for the day, we would climb all over the buildings. We made forts in the many sandlots, and it was a sad day when all vacant lots were filled with homes."

—

Sue Lundblade

"Along Lincoln Way, there were houses, but as you went on the other side of 19th Avenue, it was all sand dunes forever. Then suddenly houses began going up. They were building them during the war. Many people came then, and they decided to stay. The feel of the city changed."

—

Valerie Meehan (born 1924)

"When I was in sixth grade, they were cutting 34th Avenue through from Santiago, probably as far as Moraga. I remember that Sunset Boulevard was just cut through, connecting with the park. There were other streets that had to be cut through—all the streets on the other side of Sunset."

—

Andy Casper (born 1924)

At Wawona and 19th Avenue there was a huge hole in the ground that was used as a dump. We discovered it one day, and, scavengers that we were, we found two full unopened cases of white shoe polish. We couldn't believe our eyes! We went door to door in the neighborhood, selling them for 10 cents each."

—

Frances Larkin (born 1925)

Many Sunset houses had unfinished backyards with plenty of sand. In this photo, Gordon Gribble sits with his father, Waldron, in their backyard on 30th Avenue in the early 1940s. Gordon said, "My dad later converted the whole yard into a beautiful brick patio with planters, steps, etc."

In this 1948 photo, Larry Boysen rides his tricycle on 12th Avenue, with Golden Gate Heights in the background.

"I think I was 10 or 11 years old. All of a sudden the big focus in San Francisco was this mountain lion. No one knew how it got there or where it was. We were sneaking around in the park looking for it but hoping we didn't run into it. That went on for a couple of weeks (maybe longer) until they found it in someone's garage on 7th Avenue. The hunter tranquilized the mountain lion and took it away."

—

Fred Van Dyke (born 1929)

"As kids in the 1940s, we didn't see a lot of cars on the street. We would yell, 'Get a horse!' when the car drivers interrupted our football game on the street."

—

Thomas McCormack

"I remember when they were building houses in the late 1940s. The flat roofs of the houses were covered with tar to seal them. The workers had a trailer that melted the solid chunks of tar to be spread on the roof. We would get a solid piece that had fallen on the ground, remove the paper covering, and chew it. On reflection, I'm surprised that none of us lost any fillings or teeth."

—

Sue Lundblade

"In the '40s and '50s, many young people (including me) were taken to the Sunset by their fathers for driving lessons. The joke was that if you lost control, you could only run into a sand dune!"

—

Dorothy Bryant

"I remember when they were going to build Treasure Island. They were deciding where to build this 1939 World's Fair. The sites that I remember as a child were the sand dunes and the shoals off Yerba Buena Island. They decided that nothing was ever going to be done about the sand dunes out here, so the most viable thing was to fill in Treasure Island."

—

Valerie Meehan

"In Parkside Square, neighborhood boys and girls would play football in fall and winter, hardball in spring and summer, until the light left, the streetlights came on, and we knew we were in trouble, late for dinner, exhausted, glowing, probably not smelling too good."

—

Jerry Fleming, St. Cecilia School, Class of 1960

"I was a fifth-grade student at St. Cecilia's School when the 1957 earthquake hit. We were all herded into the recess yard after church. We weren't allowed back in the school building, and parents were called to come take us home. One boy got hysterical—knelt down, put an ear to the ground, and started screaming that he could hear 'the earth cracking and popping.' That got a lot of other kids screaming, and the nuns had to quell the impending riot."

—

Jo Anne Quinn, St. Cecilia School, Class of 1960

"A lot of Italians and Irish used to live here. Columbus Day and St. Patrick's Day were always big days. We used to have a St. Patrick's Day dinner at the church, and the Italians would show up. They'd take a couple of tables. They had a big salami and French bread. There was a lot of camaraderie between them all."

—

Joe Hurley

"We always walked home from Fleishhacker Pool to Kirkham Street, almost two miles. We walked everywhere. We didn't have a car, but in those days people walked everywhere."

—

Frances Larkin

"The neighborhood was quite different when we moved here in the 1950s. The population was different, mostly Irish. There were no Chinese restaurants. If you wanted Chinese food, you went to Chinatown. We did that for a long time. Then the area slowly evolved into this multicultural neighborhood we have now."

—

John Wentzel

"We hired drivers to deliver our handmade ice cream. When they came across a sand dune, they usually thought the truck could make it through. But the dunes were usually deeper than the drivers thought, and they'd get stuck."

—

Ellen Kieser,
former owner of Kieser's Colonial,
Irving Street near 19th Avenue

Blocks of houses stood across the street from empty sand lots in the early days of building in the Sunset.

NOTES

1. Pauline Scholten, "Neighborhoods: The Sunset," *Pacific,* August 1980, p. 38.

2. Val Golding, *SAN FRANCISCO: that was THE CITY that was,* quoted at http://www.outsidelands.org/boneyard.php.

3. "Air Views of San Francisco," *San Francisco News,* February 4, 1938, p. 16.

CHAPTER 7

GETTING FROM HERE TO THERE:

TRANSPORTATION IN THE SUNSET

The first artery that went through the Sunset District was the Central Ocean Road, a macadamized (paved) toll road that opened in May 1865. Starting approximately at Divisadero and McAllister Streets in the Western Addition, the Central Ocean Road entered the Sunset at 3rd Avenue, then zigzagged southwestward until it ended at the Ocean House roadhouse at what is now between Sloat Boulevard and Ocean Avenue, near Middlefield Drive.

The Central Ocean Road provided the only access to the middle of the Sunset District until the twentieth century. A newspaper article said of it, "The circuitous route of the road as it winds around the hills opens up a constant succession of new and beautiful views not to be found in any other drive in the county."[1]

EARLY PUBLIC TRANSIT

At the northern edge of the Sunset, Leland Stanford started a steam train line in 1883. The Park & Ocean Railroad (a subsidiary of Southern Pacific) train ran from Stanyan Street to H Street (now Lincoln Way) and along H Street to the beach, and then continued through Golden Gate Park

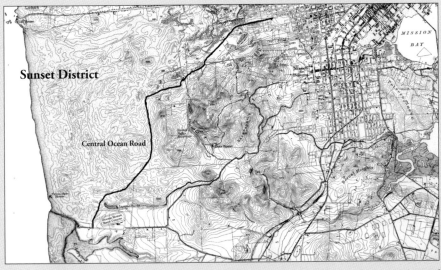

The Central Ocean Road on this 1869 U.S. Coast Survey map was the only route through the central part of the Sunset District in the 1800s.

and terminated at 49th Avenue (now La Playa) and B (now Balboa) Street. For five cents each way, San Franciscans could see parts of the city they had never seen before. Riders looking to the north saw the growing Golden Gate Park; looking south, they saw thousands of acres of sand dunes. The train had several obligatory stops, for access to Golden Gate Park, but it also had to stop randomly so that workers could sweep mounds of shifting sand off the tracks.

A steam train began running along H Street (now Lincoln Way) in 1883.

The steam train set the stage for the pattern of development of the Sunset neighborhood. Development followed the rail line, with houses scattered through the Inner Sunset and along H Street and at the beach, where wells provided residents with water.

The steam train stopped running in 1898 and was replaced by streetcars in 1898 and by electric trains in March 1899. The electric trains ran only on Sundays and holidays, using equipment rebuilt from older steam trains. The train on H Street was abandoned in the early twentieth century. However, the streetcars continued running until replaced by buses in the middle of the century.

In 1892, the Metropolitan Railway began running a streetcar line from Eddy and Market Streets to Golden Gate Park, with a branch extending from Clayton and Page Streets to the Olympic Grounds at 7th Avenue and Irving Street. For the 1894 Midwinter Fair in Golden Gate Park, this line was extended to 9th Avenue and H Street, one of the main entrances to the fair.

After the Midwinter Fair, transit companies (there were several; transit companies were not combined into one Municipal Railway until the 1940s) hoped to extend streetcar lines south from the Richmond District through the Sunset. However, Golden Gate Park superintendent John McLaren would not allow streetcars to go through the park, so the few lines that did run through the Sunset were extensions of other lines that ran downtown.

PUBLIC TRANSPORTATION IN THE TWENTIETH CENTURY

The twentieth century presented a few interesting paradoxes when it came to transit development in San Francisco. At the beginning of the 1900s, several transit companies ran lines in San Francisco. Attempting to address the problems of these competing companies, the city charter of 1900 included a city policy to work toward public ownership of all public transportation. This situation created an impediment for investors to build new rail lines and slowed the development of residential property in outlying areas such as the Sunset.

As explained on pages 26–27, Parkside Realty Company (PRC) was organized in 1905 to develop land in the southern portion of the Sunset District. Recognizing that people would move to places that had public transportation, PRC directors formed the Parkside Transit Company (PTC) in late 1906. The PTC asked the city to approve the franchise for a line that became the no. 17. Approved by the city in 1907 and built in 1908–09, the 17 line connected the growing Parkside District with downtown through a streetcar that ran from the Ferry Building down Market, through the Haight-Ashbury District, along Lincoln Way to 20th Avenue, and south on 20th. As Stan Adair remembers, "The old #17 car ran just a couple blocks from our home at 1842 18th Avenue. It cost us kids two and a half cents per ride. We bought a card for fifty cents—twenty rides—and the conductor punched the card on each ride."

At Wawona, the #17 streetcar turned east to 19th Avenue and then ran for a few blocks south on 19th to Sloat Boulevard. (On Sundays and holidays, the line continued running west on Sloat to the beach.) This is the only streetcar that ever ran on 19th Avenue in the Sunset—even if only for a few blocks. After 19th Avenue was widened in 1937, the line terminated at 19th and Wawona. The 17 line running up 20th Avenue was discontinued in 1945.

The 17 streetcar ran on 20th Avenue between Lincoln Way to Wawona Street. This streetcar has just turned right from Wawona Street to run for two blocks south on 19th Avenue.

The PTC also started running a streetcar on Taraval in 1908; this line was replaced by the L Taraval line in 1919 (see the next page).

Prior to World War II, transit anticipated development; lines were established where builders wanted to construct and sell houses. After the war, building anticipated transit, since by then development began to be centered around the use of the private automobile.

> *"When my grandparents bought their home on 19th Avenue in the 1930s, they had decided to avoid buying on 20th Avenue because of the 17 streetcar. They didn't want to live on a busy, noisy street like 20th."*
>
> —
>
> Chuck Barnhouse

> *"Four thousand acres of land available for homes to be bought within eighteen to twenty-five minutes of the heart of the city at Third, Kearny and Market streets, is the keynote of the agitation for the Twin Peaks tunnel."*
>
> —
>
> San Francisco Chronicle,
> August 13, 1910, p. 10

> *"On the day the Sunset Tunnel opened, I stood with my dad at about 20th and Judah and saw Mayor 'Sunny Jim Rolph' at the controls of the streetcar as it made its first run out in the Sunset."*
>
> —
>
> Stan Adair

> *"Let me tell you a story about 'nipping' streetcars [riding on the outside 'cow catcher,' thus avoiding paying the fare]. One day a friend and I, in a fit of careless rapture, decided to nip an N car through the Sunset Tunnel. Not a long distance to travel, but with all the noise, speed, and rattling (we called those cars 'Rattlers' in those days), both of us were hanging on for dear life. At the tunnel's end, we both staggered off, white-faced and determined never to do that again!"*
>
> —
>
> Steve Aguado

TUNNELS PROVIDE A FASTER TRIP DOWNTOWN

One of the barriers to development in the western part of San Francisco was the hills that separated the downtown business district from the Outside Lands. The Twin Peaks Tunnel was designed to provide streetcar service from downtown to the areas in the west. When the first streetcar went through the tunnel on February 4, 1918, "the Twin Peaks Property Owners Association was there to take people on guided tours of neighborhoods being developed, including St. Francis Wood, Forest Hill, Parkside, Ingleside Terrace, and Westwood Park."[2] The trip to downtown from these neighborhoods was reduced from one hour to twenty minutes, thus inspiring a boom in house building.

Starting in 1918 a shuttle bus ran down Taraval Street connecting the West Portal area with 33rd Avenue. The shuttle was replaced by the L streetcar in April 1919, and the L began running through the tunnel in 1923. The line was extended to 48th Avenue in 1923, and then to 46th Avenue and Wawona in 1937. The last terminus, still used today, brought riders to the zoo, the beach, and Fleishhacker Pool.

In 1926 work began on the Duboce Tunnel, aimed at connecting downtown to the area just south of Golden Gate Park. Streetcars entered the tunnel at Duboce Park, and exited on the west side at Cole and Carl Streets, just east of the growing Sunset District. Initially, Sunset landowners resisted the new tunnel, at least partly because the city planned to charge a property tax to pay for the tunnel's construction. Edward Treadwell, a spokesman for Sunset property owners, spoke before the board of supervisors on November 13, 1922, saying, "This measure proposes to levy an assessment of $1,600,000 on men and women who own

The Twin Peaks Tunnel opened in 1918, providing streetcar service downtown to residents on the west side of the city.

small homes and a large tract of sand dunes and sand hills, and for that reason alone the assessment is arbitrary and unjust."[3]

On the other side, Judge Daniel S. O'Brien, a 12th Avenue resident, thought the Duboce tunnel was a great idea and worked with groups to promote it. He later said, "There's nothing like stick-to-itiveness when you want anything. We went after the tunnel and we fought for it. We were determined to win and we won. When the bore is completed there will be opened up one of the most magnificent residential districts to be found anywhere in California."[4]

In 1928, the Sunset Tunnel (the Duboce name was dropped) opened to great fanfare and excitement. With another way to connect the Sunset to downtown, more developers began to grade the dunes, build streets, and build new houses south of Golden Gate Park.

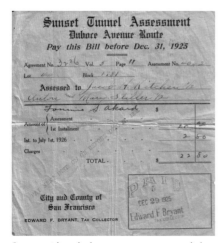

Sunset residents had to pay an assessment to help pay for the Duboce-Sunset Tunnel.

The first N Judah streetcar on the Sunset Tunnel's opening day in 1928.

In other areas of San Francisco, most lines began as trains, cable cars, or streetcars and were converted in the mid-1900s to diesel or electric-trolley bus lines. The Sunset never had cable cars and had few trains. By the time extensive transportation lines came to the Sunset, they were "motor coaches" (buses), a new technology at the time. The Sunset was the first area of the city to get motor coach service, even when the buses were feeder lines to more established streetcar lines.

Over the years, as the Sunset grew, other lines began to fill the neighborhood. Most early lines were built to connect the Sunset to downtown. For example, people traveled on various lines to Lincoln Way, where they could transfer to regular lines that ran downtown. In the early 1900s few lines connected one part of the Sunset to another part of the neighborhood—primarily because the area was so sparsely populated—but Sunset service increased in the 1940s and 1950s when the neighborhood had grown.

Streets Designed for the Automobile

Nineteenth Avenue began as a quiet, unpaved two-lane road. It was paved in the early 1900s and, by 1909, became a popular site for auto races. When the Golden Gate Bridge opened in 1937, 19th Avenue was widened to a six-lane road to provide a southern connection to the bridge. It became California State Highway 1 in the late 1930s.

As early as 1866, the city planned for a direct road along the beach connecting the west end of Golden Gate Park and Sloat Boulevard. The name *The Great Highway* first appeared on maps in the 1870s. Although the city built various roads along the beach in the late 1800s, these roads were often damaged by encroaching water and drifting sand.

Nineteenth Avenue was like a country road in 1900.

Nineteenth Avenue was widened in the 1930s to provide a direct route to the new Golden Gate Bridge. This photo, taken during the widening process, looks south from about Wawona Street. The clump of trees on the right are part of what became Sigmund Stern Grove.

After it was widened in the 1930s, 19th Avenue became a six-lane highway through the Sunset District. In 2008, the *San Francisco Chronicle* described the street as "one of the most dangerous roadways in the city."[5]

THE GREAT HIGHWAY

In 1927 the City of San Francisco began to rebuild the Great Highway, and, on June 9, 1929, it held a grand opening ceremony for the Great Highway and Ocean Beach Esplanade. Called "the broadest boulevard in the world," the new road featured underground tunnels at Sloat, Taraval, Judah, and the Beach Chalet (near Fulton) so that pedestrians could reach the beach without crossing the road.

More than 50,000 people gathered at the end of Lincoln Way to celebrate the opening of this new road designed by city engineer Michael O'Shaughnessy. Newspapers reported that the festivities

The Great Highway in 1923, before the Esplanade was created.

The completed Great Highway and Ocean Beach Esplanade in 1929.

included 1,014 musicians, with participation from the Shriners, Native Sons, ROTC, Boy Scouts, and other groups. One newspaper article proclaimed, "The little road that Adolph Sutro built in 1887 is now a magnificent stretch of boulevard, 200 feet wide and three miles long."[6]

SUNSET BOULEVARD

Sunset Boulevard runs between 36th and 37th avenues from Lake Merced to Lincoln Way. The boulevard was built in 1931 to give drivers a direct route from the south to Golden Gate Park. The large thoroughfare relieved many of the surrounding streets from traffic that increased as dependence on the automobile grew.

Before Sunset Boulevard was built, the street ended in a sand dune southwest of Grace Guildea's home on 36th Avenue.

Before building Sunset Boulevard in 1931, workers had to grade the sand dunes. This photograph was taken near Santiago Street.

Sunset Boulevard today.

THE FREEWAY REVOLT

By the 1950s, automobile traffic in San Francisco was recognized as a problem, and many people believed that the solution was to build more freeways. Proposals were primarily centered on the eastern part of the city, but they also included several freeways in the Sunset District. Most proposals were designed to connect heavily trafficked streets with the Golden Gate Bridge. During the 1950s Sunset District proposals suggested freeways along 19th Avenue, between 7th and 8th Avenues, on Hugo Street, and along the beach, where the Great Highway runs. Tunnels were also proposed below the Golden Gate Heights and West Portal neighborhoods. Whatever roadways were built would have linked up with freeways through Golden Gate Park to the Golden Gate Bridge.

In response, the now-famous San Francisco "freeway revolt" began. Neighborhood residents protested the destruction of their homes and streets for large concrete structures designed to move automobiles. Some newspapers initially supported the plan but began to oppose it over time. The freeway revolt is remembered more for preventing downtown freeways, but it affected plans throughout the city. It also spread throughout the country, to other places where freeways were being proposed as the logical solution to increasing traffic problems.

The Western Freeway, which was the general name for freeways proposed for the Sunset, was rejected by the board of supervisors in 1959, but two proposals remained, including one for a freeway that would run from the Panhandle through Golden Gate Park. A petition submitted to the board of supervisors on April 13, 1961, said:

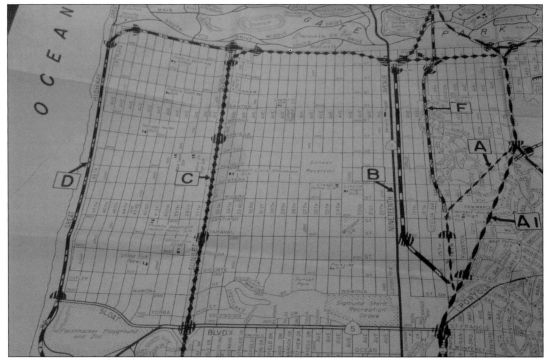

Streets that might have been affected by various 1950s proposals for changing roadways in the Sunset District. A freeway was proposed for 7th Avenue. Various other roads were to be changed to feed into underground freeways in Golden Gate Park.

> We, the undersigned property owners and voters in the Sunset District, vigorously oppose any freeway plan that will disrupt our neighborhood and petition you to vote against such a proposal. Most of us have lived in this area many years. The ties of friendship and neighborhood represent an intangible value that can in no way be compensated; nor do we feel it equitable to ask us to give up our homes and to pay exorbitant prices for comparable ones in areas removed from old and familiar associations.

The board of supervisors disapproved a revised Western Freeway plan in 1961, but some freeway proposals re-emerged in the 1960s. During a 1964 rally in the park protesting the freeway proposals, folk singer Malvina Reynolds sang "The Cement Octopus,"* a song she had written:

> There's a cement octopus sits in Sacramento, I think.
> Gets red tape to eat, gasoline taxes to drink.
> And it grows by day and it grows by night,
> And it rolls over ev'rything in sight.
> Oh, stand by me and protect that tree
> From the freeway misery …
>
> Old John MacLaren** [*sic*] won't take this lying down,
> We can hear his spirit move in the sandy ground,
> He built this Eden on the duney plain,
> Now they're making it a concrete desert again,
> Oh, stand by me and protect that tree
> From the freeway misery.

Eventually, the freeway proposals for the Sunset were abandoned; no similar proposals have emerged since the 1960s.

SUNSET RESIDENTS TRAVEL AROUND THE CITY

By the 1960s, the Sunset District was almost completely covered with streets and housing. The area had been opened up to residential structures because of the many ways transportation had come to the area. The car was everywhere, although parking spaces were still plentiful in the area. And thousands of people every day rode the many public transportation lines to workplaces elsewhere in the city. At that time, the lines that ran through the Sunset, connecting the area with others in San Francisco, included the L and N streetcar lines, as well as a number of buses: the 28, which ran on 19th Avenue north to the Presidio or south to Stonestown and the Outer Mission; the 66, which ran on Quintara Street and ended downtown; the 10, which connected Sunset residents along 9th Avenue with the Richmond District to the north and Glen Park and the Mission to the southeast; the 72, on Lincoln Way; and the 18, along Sloat Boulevard and north to Playland.

---

* "The Cement Octopus," words and music by Malvina Reynolds; copyright 1964 Schroder Music Company, renewed 1992. Used by permission.

** John McLaren was the superintendent of Golden Gate Park from 1890 to 1943.

NOTES

1. "The Drive to the Race Course," *The Bulletin*, May 20, 1865, p. 5.
2. Carolyn Loeb. *Entrepreneurial Vernacular*, p. 93.
3. "Sunset Folk Hard against Duboce Tube," *San Francisco Chronicle*, November 14, 1922, p. 3.
4. *San Francisco Chronicle*, April 25, 1925, p. 71.
5. *San Francisco Chronicle*, June 5, 2008, p. B1.
6. "Thousands Cheer as Great Ocean Esplanade Is Opened," *San Francisco Examiner*, June 10, 1929, p. 1.

The L Taraval streetcar in the 1920s.

The 7 line in 1941 turning north from Lincoln Way to enter Golden Gate Park and head toward Playland-at-the-Beach. The 7 was the only transportation line allowed to run through Golden Gate Park.

A few different streetcar styles operated at the N Judah streetcar turnaround near the beach in 1940.

CHAPTER 8

RESTRICTIVE COVENANTS:

EXCLUSION AND INCLUSION

Entire books can be written about U.S. laws that have institutionalized prejudice against racial groups. This chapter focuses on the California and San Francisco laws and attitudes that affected the Sunset District as it grew. Attitudes in San Francisco mirrored many that were prevalent around the country. For example, a large number of Chinese men came to the United States during and after the Gold Rush as prospectors, vendors, and construction workers. When the economy faltered, the federal government passed laws depriving these people of civil rights. While this was happening, San Francisco and California were passing their own laws to limit the civil rights of these groups.

ANTI-ASIAN LAWS IN SAN FRANCISCO

In 1860, San Francisco passed a law prohibiting Chinese children from attending public schools. In 1870, the board of supervisors passed an ordinance saying, "No person upon any sidewalk shall carry a basket or baskets, bag or bags, suspended from or attached to poles across or upon the shoulder,"[1] a common form of transport by Chinese peddlers. In 1873 the tax for laundry owners whose carts had two horses was $2, while a $15 tax was levied on laundries that transported clothes without using a horse.[2] (Most Chinese laundry owners did not own a horse.) In that same decade, a new law required that the sheriff cut the hair of all prisoners to one inch, thereby humiliating

An 1870 San Francisco law banned pole carriers, a common form of transport for Chinese residents.

"For nearly five years, I have had charge of the Japanese Tea Garden at Golden Gate Park. I have endeavored to perform my work to the satisfaction of all. ... All my earnings at the park have been invested in beautifying and improving the tea garden. I have, at my own expense, imported from Japan many rare trees and plants. ... I have drawn plans for the future improvement of the garden and want to be given a chance to carry this out. I appeal to you to permit me to retain my position."

—

From letter by Makoto Hagiwara to the San Francisco Park Commission, dated January 10, 1900[4]

a male Chinese prisoner by eliminating his queue, the long braided hair that represented personal identity. In 1879, the U.S. Supreme Court declared this ordinance unconstitutional.

Chinese immigrants often did dangerous work that other citizens were not willing to do. According to an 1887 newspaper article, "about half the workmen engaged in manufacturing dynamite in this state are Chinamen. They fill the most hazardous positions in the packing and mixing houses and do not receive any more pay for the work."[3] San Francisco's dynamite factories, several of which were in the Sunset, periodically exploded, severely injuring or killing Chinese workers.

Prejudice against Asians was strong in San Francisco at the beginning of the twentieth century, and few were exempt. Makoto Hagiwara, for example, had helped create the Japanese Tea Garden in Golden Gate Park for the 1894 Midwinter Fair. When the fair ended, the Hagiwara family continued to maintain and live in the garden. In 1900 they were told to leave the tea garden, and the board of park commissioners took over the garden's management from 1901 through 1907.

Undaunted, Makoto Hagiwara opened a new business, the Japanese Village (also called the New Japanese Village and Tea Garden), on H Street (now Lincoln Way) between 7th and 8th Avenues. From 1903 to 1905, the Hagiwara family ran the business and planted bushes and trees on this Inner Sunset block. (Descendents of these trees still grow in the backyards of 7th and 8th Avenue houses.) In 1907 prejudice against Asians had lessened, and Golden Gate Park Superintendent John McLaren invited the Hagiwara family to return to running the tea garden. The Hagiwaras closed the Japanese Village, and family members ran the Golden Gate Park Japanese

Tea Garden until World War II, when they were again victims of prejudice. They and other Japanese Americans were sent to internment camps when the United States was at war with Japan. The Hagiwara family never returned to Golden Gate Park.

RESTRICTIVE COVENANTS AND DEED RESTRICTIONS

Developers in the early 1900s often wrote rules and regulations into their deeds. Buyers agreed to abide by these rules, which often banned commercial businesses and regulated the size, design, and cost of homes within the development. But they also included restrictive covenants specifying that homes were not to be rented or sold to nonwhites or Jews.

When subdivisions such as St. Francis Wood (started in 1912) and Westwood Highlands (built in the 1920s) were developed, new homeowner associations were created to help enhance neighborhoods and retain the value of properties.

> One of the most important functions of the neighborhood associations … was to implement restrictive covenants. These documents were contractual agreements among property owners stating that they would not permit a non-Caucasian to own, occupy, or lease their property. Those signing the covenant bound themselves and their heirs to exclude blacks from the covered area for a specified period of time. In the event of the covenant's violation, any party to the agreement could call upon the courts for enforcement and could sue the transgressor for damages.[5]

The Sunset District had few residence communities or associations, so individual property deeds often included deed restrictions. Some Sunset builders had some form of racial restrictions in their early deeds, usually with an expiration date decades later. A person buying a home signed a contract agreeing to these restrictions.

In 1916, Fernando Nelson started building Parkway Terrace between Lincoln Way and Irving Street, from 27th to 33rd Avenue. The deed for a house on 29th Avenue read:

> Prior to the 1st day of January 1950, no trade, business or manufacturers of any kind, or anything of the nature thereof … no stable, grocery or mercantile business … at no time shall any salon be maintained or

Fernando Nelson advertised his new Parkway Terrace development as having "no Africans or Asiatics."

This 1918 ad announced that the houses to be built on 14th Avenue to 19th Avenue from Pacheco to Quintara Street were part of "A Restricted Residence District." The developer's brochure describing the project's restrictions specified, "No Africans, Asiatics or any other colored race."

conducted upon such premises. … the parties of the second part, shall not convey, lease, or rent the said premises, or a part thereof, to any person or persons of African, Asiatic or Mongolian descent, or do any act whatever which will permit such persons, or any of them, to own, lease, or rent said premises or any part thereof.[6]

An ad in the *San Francisco Chronicle* (August 1916) for Parkway Terrace listed the development's advantages, including "No Africans or Asiatics."

Often the word *restricted* was used to indicate that non-Caucasians could not live in a development. An article about growth in the Sunset in the *San Francisco Call* on May 10, 1913, reported, "Sol Getz & Sons have sold several lots on Twenty-sixth avenue between Irving (I) and Judah (J) streets to Michael Fauth, the builder, who will erect homes for sale. The lots Mr. Fauth purchased are in a restricted block and only first class buildings are being erected there."

The Stoneson Brothers built houses just south of the Sunset District. The 1939 deed for one of their houses read, "No person other than one of the White Caucasian Race shall rent, lease, use or occupy any building on any lot in said Tract, except that this Covenant shall not prevent occupancy by domestic servants of a race other than White Caucasian employed by an owner or tenant in said Tract."

Many of the deeds for houses built by Henry Doelger in 1941 included the following statement: "… said property shall not be sold, conveyed, leased, rented or occupied by any person other than one of the White or Caucasian race."[7]

Most other Sunset builders did not include racial restrictions in deeds. However, even without specific deed restrictions, unwritten and unspoken rules kept the Sunset District, and most neighborhoods in the developing Outside Lands, primarily Caucasian.

In some cases, opposition to housing integration was more open. In a letter dated May 17, 1943, to the Real Estate Association of San Francisco, the president and secretary of the Parkside District Improvement Club wrote: "We have received rumors that colored people and Filipinos were attempting to purchase property, namely new homes being erected [*sic*] in the Parkside and Sunset district. We would appreciate any information you would be able to give us and what we might do to prevent this situation from developing."[8]

Various legal cases challenged the legality of housing restrictions. In 1948, the U.S. Supreme Court ruled on restrictive covenants when deciding on *Kraemer v. Shelley*, a case that involved a black couple in St. Louis who had bought a home in a white neighborhood. After the sale the couple received a court order vacating the sale and requiring them to move. Chief Justice Fred M. Vinson wrote the decision for a unanimous court:

> The Negro petitioners entered into contracts of sale with willing sellers for the purchase of properties upon which they desired to establish homes. Solely because of their race and color they are confronted with orders of court divesting their titles in the properties and ordering that the premises be vacated. White sellers … have been enjoined from selling the properties to any Negro or colored person. Under such circumstances, to suggest that the Negro petitioners have been accorded the same rights as white citizens, to purchase, hold, and convey real property is to reject the plain meaning of language. We hold that the action of the District Court directed against the Negro purchasers and the white sellers denies rights intended by Congress to be protected by the Civil Rights Act and that, consequently the action cannot stand.[9]

After the Supreme Court ruling, restrictions no longer appeared in house deeds around the country, although racial discrimination in housing did not disappear. The unspoken "understanding" that white neighborhoods would remain white continued.

"I'm sure there was discrimination, but we never discriminated. God, we were glad to rent. In fact, we had these apartments on Taraval Street. This black couple came up and said they were interested. I said that was fine and I took them out there. I kept bugging the couple. I'd call them and say, 'You were interested. Would you like to move in soon?' We never heard from them again. I think they were just testing us."

—

Ray Galli Jr., son of builder R. F. Galli

"I am a Negro veteran. I have been trying to buy a new house. One that they sell to veterans. I have been refused because I am an American Negro. The Standard Builders and Galli Builders say they cannot sell to me because I am a Negro."

—

From a 1949 letter by San Franciscan Lionel Wheeler to President Harry Truman, quoted in Deirdre Sullivan, *Letting Down the Bars*

"In 1958, when we moved into this house on 20th Avenue near Noriega, we were the only Asians on the block and almost the only Asians in the area. There was one Asian family in the next block."

—

Mamie Moy

THE FEDERAL HOUSING ADMINISTRATION (FHA)

During the Great Depression of the 1930s, many people lost their homes to foreclosure. Many others could not consider buying a home because of high costs. At that time, people taking out home loans, often for 50 percent of the cost of the house, had to pay the full amount of the loan in three to five years.

In 1934, Congress passed the Federal Housing Act, establishing the Federal Housing Administration (FHA), which provided mortgage insurance and a new way for people to buy homes. Through FHA, people could borrow 80 to 90 percent of their home costs and spread payments over twenty-five to thirty years. The long-term, low-rate mortgage replaced the short-term, high-rate loan.

HOME BUILDERS

DOELGER BUILT HOMES, 8-4350 AND UP—FHA TERMS
HENRY DOELGER
San Francisco's Largest Home Builder
330 Judah Street   OVerland 3100

GALLI BUILT MEANS "BETTER BILT"
"ASK THE OWNER OF A GALLI BUILT HOME"
R. F. GALLI, Builder
877 West Portal Ave.   OVerland 0850 and 7921

Ads in the *San Francisco Chronicle* touted FDA terms.

However, FHA made mortgage insurance available mostly to new developments that were usually sold to Caucasians in suburban areas. (Although located within the San Francisco city limits, the Sunset was considered a suburb.) Sunset builders' advertisements touted "FHA terms," and FHA loans helped the Sunset grow.

Moreover, the FHA encouraged restricting neighborhood businesses and diversity, even after the 1948 Supreme Court ruling. "FHA manuals specifically warned of the detrimental effect of racial change. Up until 1948, when the Supreme Court struck down their use, FHA supplied lenders with a form for racially restrictive covenants required on the properties which it insured."[10]

In the 1950s, some groups in San Francisco began to show concern about the unequal right to housing. A document published by the Council for Civic Unity of San Francisco stated, "Equal opportunity in the search for shelter does not exist in San Francisco. A white family with sufficient financial resources can rent or buy a home wherever it chooses. A nonwhite family, regardless of income, does not have free access to this city's housing."[11]

WILLIE BROWN AND STANDARD BUILDING COMPANY

Standard Building Company, which had built houses in the Sunset, ran into trouble in May 1961, when sales agents refused to show a model home in the Forest Knolls development to Willie Brown, a then-unknown twenty-seven-year-old black lawyer. Brown later wrote, "My wife, Blanche, and her girlfriend … went up to look at a house on Forest Hills—Forest Knolls. It was called Sunstream Homes. And the people showing the house at that time saw them coming, and they abandoned the model home. … And we, of course, alerted the press, and the first … sit-in demonstration in San

Francisco occurred, generated because they wouldn't show my wife a home."[12]

The NAACP set up picket lines at the entrance to Forest Knolls and outside the Sunstream Homes office on 19th Avenue in the Sunset. Demonstrators held signs reading "Is the customer always white?" and "Apartheid or Brotherhood."

San Francisco Mayor George Christopher was quoted in a San Francisco newspaper saying

Demonstrators protested on 19th Avenue against Standard Building Company's policy of not showing homes or selling to black people.

he "knew of no law requiring an owner to sell a house to any one he didn't want to deal with."[13] As the story continued to grow, however, the mayor encouraged the Gellerts, owners of Standard Building Company, to show the house to the Browns.

When the Gellerts agreed to give the Browns a tour of the house, a spokesperson added, "We have not sold in the past to Negroes and the

"I had a letter in my hand from Dean Fleming verifying me as a member of the [UCSF School of Dentistry] faculty saying he's clean and he's decent, he's an upright citizen, please help him. And I carried that letter around I guess 20 or 30 places where I saw signs around the university … wherever I saw signs for rent. And as soon as I'd show my face, 'No, I can't rent to you. No, people wouldn't like it,' or whatever."

—

Daniel Collins,
quoted in Paul T. Miller,
The Postwar Struggle for Civil Rights

"When we moved to San Francisco, Chinese people were not allowed to own property. We rented an apartment on Jackson Street. The law changed in the 1940s, and we decided to look for a house in the 1950s. When we told our friends that we were looking for a house outside the area, they were skeptical that we could find anything, but we were too naïve to think we wouldn't. It was a revelation to us that property was so restricted."

—

Woody Moy

"My family lived in an all-white neighborhood on 19th Avenue in the 1940s. There was one black family, and they got persecuted. They lived right next door. All the great white people were out to get rid of them. Mostly the white people would ignore them. They wouldn't accept them as human beings."

—

Fred Van Dyke

question of selling to Negroes in the future is still under advisement."[14] Willie Brown declined the offer to tour the house, saying, "I won't see it unless the Standard Building Company makes a policy statement to the effect that it will show homes in its tracts to the highest qualified buyers regardless of race or color."[15] Willie Brown later served as speaker of the California Assembly and then as mayor of San Francisco.

THE STRUGGLE FOR CHANGE

In the mid-1900s, nonwhite citizens began to move to the Sunset District, despite objections by Caucasians. In 1952, when an African American talked about buying a house that was for sale on 16th Avenue, the owner received an anonymous letter saying, "For your own good, don't sell to colored." The owner's response was that she was "selling the house to anyone who cares to buy it."[16]

In 1957 Audley and Josephine Cole (see chapter 9) bought a house at 36th Avenue and Lawton Street. The couple lived there for the rest of their lives, into the twenty-first century, with no publicized difficulties. In contrast, Richard and Patricia Dixon moved to Kirkham Street near the Great Highway in 1962. A few weeks after moving in, the couple found graffiti on their garage door: "Nigger go home, KKK." Some neighbors said, "I can't help thinking they brought it on themselves moving into an all-white neighborhood" and "I don't think they're on our level. I just think they would be happier living among their own people." However, another neighbor said, "They seem like nice people. My children play with theirs."[17]

ETHNIC ATTITUDES IN THE SUNSET

In 1964 approximately 74 percent of San Franciscans were classified as white. According to an article in the *San Francisco Chronicle,* the Sunset had the greatest concentration of white residents, 85.8 percent.

The year before, the *San Francisco Progress* surveyed residents in city neighborhoods. One survey question asked, "In your neighborhood are people of all races and religions welcome?" The newspaper reported that in the Sunset "almost as many people said they were against minority groups moving in as said they were for them."[18] The survey separated the Sunset responses into two groups: Sunset and Parkside (approximately south of Ortega Street). The Parkside was the only area in which the combined "no" and "maybe" answers outnumbered the "yes" answers. Comments included, "All except Negroes," "I do not think Negroes would be welcome," and "Integration is slowly being accepted here."

One person in the 2500 block of 29th Avenue stated, "We are prepared to move to an all-white area if the racial pattern should ever change."[19]

Of course, not all Parkside residents believed that the area should be segregated. Mrs. William Arthur Anderson wrote, "I should like to think all races are welcome; I feel too great a homogeneity is not good for our children. They need to know all kinds of people."[20]

In 1959 the California legislature passed the Civil Rights Act. Authored by Assemblyman Jesse Unruh, the act "outlawed discrimination on the basis of race, color, religion, ancestry or national origin in all business establishments." In 1963 the Rumford Fair Housing Act, introduced by Assemblyman Byron Rumford, passed the California legislature. The bill outlawed housing discrimination, except in owner-occupied buildings with fewer than four units. It also "outlawed racial discrimination by banks, real estate brokers, mortgage companies, and other financial institutions."[21]

Outraged, a group made up of California realtors and developers collected signatures to put the issue on the state ballot. Proposition 14 would have repealed the Rumford Act and added the following amendment to the California Constitution:

> Neither the State nor any subdivision or agency thereof shall deny, limit, or abridge, directly or indirectly, the right of any person, who is willing or desires to sell, lease or rent any part or all of his real property, to decline to sell, lease or rent such property to such person or persons as he, in his absolute discretion, chooses.

This ad ran in the October 11–12, 1964, issue of the *San Francisco Progress.*

"I remember when the first Chinese family moved to our area of the Sunset in 1962 or 1963. The old Irish went nuts. It was so foreign to some of the people living here to have Chinese people living in their neighborhood."

—

Valerie Schmalz

"Terry Francois, who was black, couldn't get his children into St. Cecilia School. Mr. Francois came to my dad and asked for help. Dad, I'm sure, said 'No problem,' but the monsignor said no! The Francois children, who lived next door to me, ended up at St. Anne's."

—

Tom O'Toole, St. Cecilia School, class of 1960

"I went to St. Ignatius High School 1981 to 1985. I used to walk home every day from school and often saw Mr. Cole [an African American] outside taking care of his landscaping. He once told me that when he and Mrs. Cole first moved in, the neighbors sent him a letter asking him to move and saying that they did not want him and his wife living there. How many neighbors signed it, I don't know. He told me that Mrs. Cole was very upset and angry about it. He said he just tried to keep calm. He also said that he never had any intention of moving."

—

Arthur Pira

*"I was in the twelfth grade in 1964 when Proposition 14 was on the ballot.
It was a huge issue at that time, when discrimination was rampant.
I remember hearing all the nos in church but after mass the yeses from the adults in my neighborhood. The priests were preaching against Proposition 14 and my neighbors (who attended mass at St. Cecilia's every Sunday) didn't agree with them."*

—

Kathy Klingenberg,
St. Cecilia School,
Class of 1960

*"In late 1963 or early 1964, my fifth-grade daughter came home from school with a letter that encouraged parents to sign a petition to oppose allowing black students to attend Parkside School.
I refused to sign and wrote an angry letter back saying essentially that my children started each day saying the Pledge of Allegiance with 'freedom and justice for all.' I wrote that I couldn't sign anything that violated that. But I believe I was in the minority."*

—

Dorothy Bryant

In November 1964, Proposition 14 passed statewide by a vote of almost two to one, 4.5 million to 2.4 million. The vote in San Francisco was much closer, roughly 53 percent yes to 47 percent no. But Sunset District voters reflected the attitude of the state electorate: the vote in the Sunset was two to one in favor of the amendment. In addition, according to analyst Dr. Ralph Lane, "There were more people in the Sunset who voted on the measure than anywhere else in the city— 70 per cent compared with 55 per cent."[22]

The popular vote was overturned by the California Supreme Court in 1966. The U.S. Supreme Court agreed in 1967, saying that the amendment created "a constitutional right to discriminate on racial grounds in the sale and rental of real property," a violation of the equal protection rights guaranteed in the Fourteenth Amendment to the U.S. Constitution.

CHANGES BEGIN

The demographic makeup of the Sunset—and of the city as a whole—continually changes. The author's grandmother, the first American-born child in her Italian immigrant family, grew up in North Beach and saw buying a duplex in the Mission District as a step up. Her son and daughter-in-law grew up in the Mission District, but as they prepared to welcome their second child in 1952, they bought a house on 22nd Avenue in the Sunset, seeking an affordable neighborhood with good schools.

When the Sunset District began to develop, its residents were primarily Caucasian—Irish, Italian, and Russian immigrants. By the mid-1900s, the area had a reputation for being the home of San Francisco policemen and firemen, who were required to live within the city limits and, because of racially discriminatory practices, were of white, European heritage.

Immigration from Hong Kong and China began to increase in 1965, and many of these immigrants moved to the Sunset and Richmond Districts. Other ethnic and racial groups began moving to the Sunset in the 1970s, and the demographics of the neighborhood began to change markedly. Drive down Sunset District streets now, and you will see a diversity of businesses and people, with the largest group being Chinese.

In the neighborhood's early years, "moving up" in San Francisco meant buying a house in the Sunset District. By the end of the twentieth century, many Sunset residents were "moving up" by departing the city entirely, leaving room for others to move to the Sunset in their stead.

NOTES

1. San Francisco Municipal Reports, 1870, p. 31.

2. Author unknown, "All Persons Born or Naturalized … The Legacy of *U.S. v. Wong Kim Ark*," UC Hastings College of the Law Library, Summer 2001.

3. "Dynamite," *Daily Morning Call,* March 14, 1887, p. 3.

4. Raymond H. Clary, *The Making of Golden Gate Park, The Early Years: 1865–1906*, p. 118.

5. Douglas S. Massey and Nancy A. Denton, *American Apartheid: Segregation and the Making of the Underclass,* p. 36.

6. Property deed for "Outside Lands, Block 645 (Vol. 927, page 199, 29th Avenue). Dated April 19, 1916. The same statement appears in other original property deeds, including deeds for a house on the north side of Moraga Street between 43rd and 44th Avenue (11-5-41), 32nd Avenue between Noriega and Ortega (10-5-41), and 42nd Avenue between Moraga and Noriega (10-28-41).

7. Property deed for 1901 29th Avenue notarized January 3, 1940 and registered with the City and County of San Francisco on January 7, 1940. (Courtesy of Joyce Bauer and Ken Englund.) Research in the San Francisco Assessor's Office showed that this was a "boilerplate" statement in many Doelger deeds. A random check of Galli and Gellert houses in the Sunset showed no racial restrictions in Galli or Gellert deeds.

8. A carbon copy of this letter is in the Western Neighborhoods Project files.

9. Clement E. Vose, *Caucasians Only: The Supreme Court, the NAACP, and the Restrictive Covenant Cases,* p. 209.

10. Calvin Bradford, "Financing Home Ownership: The Federal Role in Neighborhood Decline," March 1979, p. 324.

11. Council for Civic Unity of San Francisco, *San Francisco's Housing Market—Open or Closed?,* p. 9.

12. Willie Brown, "Mayor Willie Brown Reminisces."

13. *San Francisco News-Call Bulletin,* June 2, 1961, p. 6.

14. "Tract Owner Says Negro May Look," *San Francisco Chronicle,* June 3, 1961, p. 1. According to the *Sun-Reporter* on June 24, 1961 (p. 4), the mayor spoke to Carl Gellert "who informed the mayor that Standard did not sell homes to Negroes but 'We have the matter under advisement.'"

15. Ibid.

16. "Pastor Looks at House: Woman Warned Not to Sell to Negroes," the *Sun-Reporter,* November 29, 1952, p. 1.

17. "Vandals and a Negro Home in the Sunset," *San Francisco Chronicle,* October 25, 1962, p. 10.

18. "Rating Poll: What They Said—The Sunset and Nearby Areas," *San Francisco Progress,* September 18–19, 1963, p. 4.

19. "Rating Poll: What They Said—The Parkside and Nearby Sections," *San Francisco Progress,* September 11–12, 1963, p. 11.

20, Bob Juran, "Residents Speak Out on Racial Integration," *San Francisco Progress,* May 1–2, 1963, p. 3.

21. Elaine Elinson and Stan Yogi, *Wherever There's a Fight: How Runaway Slaves, Suffragists, Immigrants, Strikers, and Poets Shaped Civil Liberties in California,* p. 148.

22. "Analysis of City's Vote on Proposition 14," *San Francisco Chronicle,* November 29, 1964, p. 15.

This aerial view of the Parkside District in 1941 shows that many blocks were covered with houses, but some of the original sand dunes stood almost untouched. Sunset Boulevard runs along the bottom of the photograph. The large flat-topped structure near the top left of the photograph is the first phase of the Sunset Reservoir. The building at the top center is the new Abraham Lincoln High School, which had opened the previous fall.

Chapter 9

Notable People

This chapter provides in-depth profiles of four people who seem to have been forgotten but who made important contributions to the history of San Francisco and the Sunset: Carl Larsen, Alice Marble, Raymond Schiller, and Josephine Cole. A number of other Sunset residents are discussed briefly at the end of the chapter.

Carl G. Larsen:
The Gentle Dane (1844–1928)

Carl Larsen

In the late 1800s, speculators began buying land in the Sunset District. One of the largest landowners, Carl Larsen, had additional ties to the district. Sometimes called the "Gentle Dane," Carl Gustav Larsen was born in 1844 in Odense, Denmark. He came to San Francisco in his late twenties and worked as a carpenter. In 1879, he started the popular Tivoli Café downtown on Eddy Street. When the café was destroyed in the earthquake and fire of 1906, Larsen was undaunted; he rebuilt it and built the new Hotel Larsen as well, where he lived.

Larsen's first venture into real estate was in 1888, when he bought one block in the Sunset at an auction. The area was still dominated by sand dunes and was largely inaccessible. He continued to buy land in the Sunset, and by 1910 he owned fourteen entire city blocks and scattered lots that totaled about nine more blocks. By the 1920s he owned substantial land in the fledgling Golden Gate Heights area, including the lots on 15th Avenue where Henry Doelger built houses in the 1930s. (See chapter 5.)

As time passed, Larsen developed, sold, or donated parts of his holdings. Well-known structures that sit on land once owned by Larsen include St. Cecilia Catholic Church on Vicente Street and the (former) Shriners Hospital on 19th Avenue.

Larsen's Chicken Ranch

In addition to his other activities, in 1890 Larsen began operating a chicken ranch on one square block bounded by 16th and 17th Avenues and Moraga and Noriega Streets. In 1905 Carl Christian Dahlgren painted a colorful depiction of the chicken ranch surrounded by Sunset sand

*"My grandfather knew Carl Larsen.
Mr. Larsen wanted him to consider
buying land out here. My grandmother
said, 'You're nuts! No one will live out in
the fog and sand and wind.'"*

—

Larry Boysen

*"All the fresh eggs, the chickens and some
of the produce used at the restaurant were
grown at the ranch. The food scraps from
the eating house were brought back to the
ranch to feed the chickens. Every morning
about four o'clock one of the ranchhands
would start out with the loaded wagon
heading for downtown. Tracing the route
of this excursion on a map shows that it
was a long, tedious, tiresome trip to the
central part of the city. The return journey
would bring them back to the ranch about
five in the evening."*

—

Stan Adair,
Spell Hippopotamus, p. 58

*"My grandparents lived on 17th Avenue
when my mother was little. My grandfather would go across the street and up a
few blocks to Larsen's farm and come back
with a chicken for dinner."*

—

Anita Brew

dunes (see this book's inside back cover). Each morning, a horse-drawn carriage took eggs from the chicken ranch to the Tivoli Café, probably using the Sunset's Central Ocean Road. Tivoli Café ads boasted, "Fresh eggs from Sunset Ranch every day."

Once a year, at Easter time, the Larsen chicken ranch hosted a large party for the neighborhood, with open bars and long tables of food. Some reports say that these annual parties got out of hand and were discontinued in 1913.[1]

According to George Stanton, a Sunset resident at the time:

> Carl Larsen would sponsor an Easter Sunday Festival at that Ranch. It was open house for all his friends and neighbors in the Sunset District. ... There was a long table on the north side and a 30 foot bar on the south side of the ranch grounds. On that table were platters and platters of hard-boiled eggs, sandwiches and every kind of cake and cookie the kids could wish for. ... There were always at least 15 to 20 barrels of beer, with three barrels going at once at the bar. Hard liquor was also served. ... Everything was free on that day. ... But news of the event eventually got out to some unsavory characters. The drunks and winos from all over town started to gather at the gate ... They all made pigs of themselves at the bar. ... Around 4:00 pm the road down from 17th Avenue to 19th Avenue was strewn with about six or seven drunks sprawled out in the middle of the road and in the gutter. ... Poor Larsen was so disturbed over what had happened that day, that he put an ad in the local papers apologizing for the conduct of those few disgusting drunks who had caused all that trouble. The ad also informed everyone that the affair would never be held again.

This image looks west across the Sunset around 1898. Carl Larsen's chicken ranch appears in the center. Note Golden Gate Park on the right side, with the Dutch windmill at the far end and the Cliff House in the far distance.

SUNSET ACTIVISM

Larsen lived downtown, but he was very involved in the Sunset. He was a member of the Nineteenth Avenue Boulevard Club, a neighborhood group that lobbied for a macadamized road and beautification along 19th Avenue. He was a member of the Sunset District Improvement Club, which raised money in 1900 to plant "bunch grass" on the west side of the newly macadamized 19th Avenue. He also worked for civic improvements and streetcar service to the area.

Larsen was not always happy when his efforts were successful. When the Twin Peaks Tunnel was being built, a tax assessment was levied on Sunset landowners, the people who would benefit most from the tunnel's construction. What happened at this point is not clear. According to the *San Francisco Chronicle,* Larsen owed about $60,000 in taxes and filed an unsuccessful protest with the city. The newspaper said that to pay his assessment Larsen sold many of his lots in May 1914.[2] However, San Francisco Block Books from 1915 and 1920 show Larsen still owning most of the Sunset land he held in 1910. In *More Parkside Pranks and Sunset Stunts,* George Stanton says that Larsen did not have enough money to pay the Twin Peaks Tunnel assessment and "died a broken hearted man." According to the *San Francisco Chronicle,* however, the Larsen estate was worth close to $800,000 when he died in 1928.

"The road to the [Larsen] Ranch from 19th Avenue was up Noriega Street. It was a very steep one-way red rock road. ... There was no car line on 20th Avenue as yet. Carl Larsen's friends from downtown had to get off the street car at 19th Avenue and Lincoln Way then walk up 19th to get to the Ranch. It was an awesome climb."

—

George Stanton in
Mary Ada Williams, *More Parkside Pranks and Sunset Stunts,* p. 74

*"I remember when the Navy put that blue jet fighter in Larsen Park. We all went there after school, and kids were there with screwdrivers, wrenches, and hammers, taking everything they could get off.
After a few days the nosecone was missing. It turned up miraculously in the house of one of my friends."*

—

John Murphy, St. Cecilia School,
Class of 1960

A GENEROUS MAN

Larsen is best remembered as the donor of Carl Larsen Park, two square blocks between 19th and 20th Avenues, between Ulloa and Wawona Streets. The original park was designed with two spaces set aside as "out-of-door card rooms," one for men and the other for women.[3] The original card rooms and soccer field are long gone, but the tennis court and baseball diamond remain, now accompanied by a basketball court, large grassy meadows, and the Charlie Sava (formerly Larsen) swimming pool. In the 1950s and 1960s, Sunset residents swam in the "modern" Larsen Pool and climbed in and around a Navy jet (one of several that sat on the land for years), a unique life-size toy for children.

In 1926, when Larsen donated this park to the city, Mayor James Rolph thanked him on the steps of City Hall, proclaiming that Larsen would "be remembered in company with other benefactors, who have accumulated great wealth within our boundaries and were inspired to reciprocate with gifts to the commonwealth."[4] A bronze plaque at Larsen Park reads, "Carl G. Larsen has generously given these two blocks to the city of San Francisco for park pleasure purposes." (The plaque was sculpted by Melvin Earl Cummings, who

Children climbed over and through the jet(s) that sat in Larsen Park in the 1950s through the 1980s.

also sculpted Sather Gate on the campus of the University of California, Berkeley.)

Two years before giving Larsen Park to San Francisco, Larsen donated land at the southern edge of Golden Gate Heights. Golden Gate Heights Park (also known as Larsen's Peak) stands on 12th to 14th Avenues, Pacheco to Quintara Streets. At 725 feet above sea level, it is one of the highest hills in San Francisco.

On October 4, 1926, Mayor James Rolph (left) formally thanked Carl Larsen for donating the land that became Larsen Park. Note that Larsen is holding a bouquet of dahlias, which had just been named the official flower of San Francisco.

In 1928 the City of San Francisco considered building a reservoir on this spot, and Larsen objected. A week before his death, he spoke to the board of supervisors:

I do feel aggrieved that they have asked me to make a reservoir out of the property, as that is fartherest [sic] from my thoughts. When I made this gift I was assured that this would be made a public park. ... Gentlemen, I am getting old; my years are numbered and I would like to see that park laid out. I would like to see the grass, the trees and the flowers that I have pictured so many times and for so many years. It has been the fondest hope of my life to see a beautiful park on those rocks and sand hills.[5]

Golden Gate Heights Park (the trees at the top of the hill), taken from the grounds of Larsen Park on 19th Avenue.

*"Larsen never discharged a man.
No matter how old they got, they were kept
on the job and finally retired.
He fed the poor, no man or woman,
hungry and without money, was ever
refused a good hot meal at the Tivoli.
Only a few years ago, a syndicate
wanted to buy that Eddy street site for a
million dollar theater. 'What will become
of my boys?' said Larsen.
'No, not while I live will I sell the Tivoli
and leave my boys out of a job.'"*

—

Andrew J. Gallagher,
San Francisco supervisor,
San Francisco Chronicle,
November 6, 1928

LARSEN'S DEATH AND DISPUTED WILL

Carl Larsen died on November 5, 1928. He was remembered for his generosity both to the City of San Francisco and to his employees at the Tivoli Café. Newspapers reported that although the café had been losing money for years before Larsen's death, he would not close the cafe or terminate any workers.

Larsen never married and had no known children. Evidence indicates that he planned to leave some of his estate to San Francisco. A handwritten will, dated July 27, 1909, and found after his death, gave $25,000 to Knud M. Truelsen, his "lifelong friend and partner in the Tivoli Café"; $10,000 to his brother Ferdinand; $5,000 each to his other brothers and a sister; and $5,000 to San Francisco orphanages. The Tivoli Café was to go to his brother Alfred. (The café closed shortly after Carl's death.) The will gave the remainder of the estate, estimated at more than $500,000, to San Francisco for a museum in Golden Gate Park.[6]

Some of the people listed in the will never saw those funds. When the will was discovered, Larsen's signature and the signature of a witness had been "cut off." Led by Agnes Marie Hunderup and Valborg Irene Vagner, grandchildren of Larsen's sister, a group of sixteen to twenty-two family members (most living in Denmark) contested the will. In 1931 Superior Court Judge Dunne declared it invalid. Truelsen initially filed a response to the heirs' claim but withdrew it after receiving a "substantial settlement" from the estate. The rest of the estate was divided among Larsen's relatives.[7]

Larsen's museum was never built in Golden Gate Park, but two Sunset parks—Golden Gate Heights Park and Larsen Park—stand as reminders of the Gentle Dane.

ALICE MARBLE: TENNIS CHAMPION, UNDERCOVER SPY, AND MORE (1913–1990)

Probably the best-known sports star to come from the Sunset District, Alice Marble, was a great tennis player whose life story had more twists and turns than many movie scripts.

Marble was born on September 28, 1913, in the northern California town of Beckwith (later changed to Beckwourth). Her family moved to 1619 12th Avenue in San Francisco's Inner Sunset when Alice was five.

As a young child, Marble was always interested in sports, especially baseball. When she was thirteen years old, she and her brother Tim attended San Francisco Seals games, going early "so we could play catch in the bleachers before the game," she wrote in her memoir. One day, thinking she was a boy, a player asked her to play catch with him. "I kept expecting someone to tell me to leave," Marble wrote. Instead, she was asked to shag flies for some of the players. Before long, local newspapers were printing stories about the new "Seals mascot." A *San Francisco Examiner* sportswriter called Marble the "Little Queen of Swat."[8]

Alice Marble.

"My brother Charles knew everyone around 12th Avenue. Alice Marble used to hit balls against the large wall in the yard at Columbus School. She drew a chalk line to indicate the width and height of tennis courts. She let Charles use her old tennis racket and play against the wall she used."

—

Catherine Murphy

LEARNING TO PLAY TENNIS

Baseball was a boys' game in those days. When Alice was thirteen years old, her brother Dan gave her a tennis racket, saying, "You can't keep hanging around the ballpark, and hitting balls through people's windows . . . and acting like a boy." At first, Marble was devastated to lose her time with the Seals, but she learned to love tennis—and to play it well. She began practicing and playing matches in Golden Gate Park.

Marble excelled at several sports, earning seven varsity letters in track, softball, soccer, and basketball while attending Polytechnic High School, just east of the Inner Sunset. Two traumatic events devastated her as a child, however: while roller skating, she watched as a friend was crushed under the wheels of a streetcar, and one evening she was raped as she left Golden Gate Park after playing tennis.

Lefty O'Doul and Alice Marble posed for this photo in 1938.

In those days, tennis was a wealthy person's game, and the Marbles were poor. Alice had opportunities to play in matches but had little money for clothing, travel, and supplies. Odd jobs and an anonymous gift enabled her to participate in her newly adopted sport.

In 1932, Marble won California State and Pacific Coast women's singles titles and was ranked seventh in the nation. With her increasing tennis successes, she came to know various Hollywood stars, including Marion Davies, Charlie Chaplin, Bing Crosby, and Carole Lombard. She was a favorite of William Randolph Hearst and often spent time at Hearst Castle in San Simeon.

THE TENNIS CHAMPION PREVAILS

In an unexpected setback, Marble collapsed during the French championship on May 24, 1934. She was diagnosed with pleurisy, then tuberculosis, and was told that she would never play tennis again. She was confined to a sanitarium in Monrovia, California, for eight months.

Marble recovered completely and returned to competition in 1935, winning the California state championship. She won the U.S. singles title in 1936 and went on to win many other awards, including her first Wimbledon title in 1939. She became the number one women's tennis player in the United States, setting a record that lasted for twenty-eight years and was ranked the world's top woman tennis player from 1936 to 1949. In the 1940s, she won seventy-one tournaments and twenty-two championships.

In 1942, Marble married Joe Crowley, a soldier sent to fight in World War II. She lost their child when she was five months pregnant, and then learned that her husband had been killed in action. She survived a suicide attempt and went on to play tennis and win tournaments.

WORLD WAR II ESPIONAGE

Alice Marble's story contains more than personal tragedies and tennis victories. According to her memoir, during World War II the U.S. government asked her to spy on Hans Steinmetz, a Nazi sympathizer who had been her lover years before. The U.S. government believed that Steinmetz was storing art and other valuables stolen by the Nazis from Jewish citizens. Marble's task was to photograph the artwork. She lived with Steinmetz in Switzerland in early 1945 and played the part of the devoted lover.

One night when Steinmetz was out, Marble photographed the art pieces. When she met with her American contact, she knew something was wrong when he demanded that she turn over the camera and film to him. Marble refused and ran into the woods. The contact (a double agent) shot her in the back. Amazingly, she survived with little permanent damage, but the film had been destroyed. However, Marble was able to recall and describe to American authorities much of the art she had seen in the basement vault of Steinmetz's chateau.

Marble was also an outspoken advocate for fairness in tennis. In July 1950, she wrote an open letter that was published in *World Tennis* magazine. The letter criticized the American Lawn Tennis Association for not allowing Althea Gibson to play in the Forest Hills tennis tournament because she was black. Marble wrote, "If tennis is a game for ladies and gentlemen, it's also time we acted a little more like gentlepeople and less like sanctimonious hypocrites. ... If Althea Gibson represents a challenge to the present crop of women players, it's only fair that they should meet that challenge on the courts." Marble said that if Gibson were not given the opportunity to compete, "then there is an uneradicable [*sic*] mark against a game to which I have devoted most of my life, and I would be bitterly ashamed." Gibson was invited to enter the 1950 U.S. championships, becoming the first African American player to compete in a Grand Slam event.

Marble spent her remaining years lecturing, teaching, playing exhibition tennis matches, and painting. In the 1950s, she had a cameo role in the Spencer Tracy/Katharine Hepburn movie *Pat and Mike*. During her tennis career, she won the U.S. singles title four times, the U.S. Open twelve times, and Wimbledon titles five times. Marble was inducted into the Tennis Hall of Fame in 1964 and the International Sportsman Hall of Fame in 1967. Although she left San Francisco early in her career, she is memorialized in the city by the Alice Marble Tennis Courts on Russian Hill. She died in December 1990.

Ray Schiller

RAYMOND SCHILLER: "MAYOR OF THE PARKSIDE" (1895–1949)

One of the most active community advocates in San Francisco was the Parkside's Raymond "Ray" Schiller, whose constant work for neighborhood improvements earned him the title "Mayor of the Parkside."

Ray Schiller was born south of Market Street in 1895. The Schillers, like many other families, moved out of the South of Market neighborhood after the 1906 earthquake and fire. In his late twenties, Schiller began his years of activism as a charter member of the South of Market Boys Club (SOMB), a community group founded in November 1924. Members were men born "south of the slot" who moved away from their neighborhood after the 1906 earthquake and fire.

SOMB members and their spouses met regularly to swap stories about their former neighborhood and to plan social and charitable events.

On September 9, 1920, Ray Schiller married Mary Louise Trade. They had three children, Rita, William, and Mary Louise (Mary Lou). In 1929 the family moved to 2422 25th Avenue. That same year, after more than twenty years of working for Malm Luggage, Schiller was laid off, a casualty of the stock market crash and the Great Depression. He started a business in the garage of his Parkside home making,

The Schillers lived on 25th Avenue in the Parkside.

selling, and repairing luggage, cases, and purses. His luggage-making skills were soon renowned.

PARKSIDE IMPROVEMENT CLUB

The Parkside Improvement Club was an all-male neighborhood advocacy group founded in 1908, when few people lived in the neighborhood. Basic services now taken for granted, such as streetlights, paved roads, postal service, schools, and public transportation, did not exist in the Parkside at the time.

Ray Schiller made and sold luggage out of his garage. He was also known for his wall of photos of politicians and other famous people at Bay Area events.

Schiller became an active member of the Parkside Improvement Club in the 1930s. He helped reorganize the club to admit women and change its name to the Parkside District Improvement Club (PDIC). Schiller served as vice president of the PDIC in 1936, then president in 1937, 1938, and 1939. As president, Schiller was often the spokesman for the club, and during this period he became known as the unofficial "Mayor of the Parkside."

Over the years the PDIC became a strong lobbying force,

and many of its proposals were adopted by the city. During Schiller's tenure, some of the projects the group advocated were

- Increasing public transportation to the area and improving street lighting

- Cutting through and paving streets for development and easy access

- Extending the terminus for the L streetcar line from 48th and Taraval to 46th and Wawona, closer to Fleishhacker Zoo and Pool

- Increasing public transportation in the Parkside area

- Removing streetcar tracks after the 17 line was discontinued on 20th Avenue

- Constructing a public high school for neighborhood youth

- Building a public library in the neighborhood

Schiller did what he could to draw attention to the Parkside neighborhood. When McCoppin Square Park was formally dedicated on August 25, 1935, Schiller was the general chairman and master of ceremonies for the event, which featured a mile-long parade that started at West Portal School and snaked down Taraval Street to McCoppin Square. The dedication ceremonies drew an estimated 10,000 people and included a tennis match, a baseball game, and a dedication address given by Mayor Angelo Rossi. Dedication committee members included city benefactors Herbert Fleishhacker, Rosalie (Mrs. Sigmund) Stern, and John McLaren.

On May 1, 1939, Schiller established the annual May Day celebration in McCoppin Square. May Day in the Parkside was a child-oriented celebration that featured young girls in their

prettiest dresses, with maypole dancing and other festivities. Each year, the mayor or another civic dignitary crowned a "May Day Queen." (In 1962 the May Day celebration moved from McCoppin Square to Parkside Square, where it continued into the 1970s.) Schiller also started an annual Halloween parade on Taraval Street for neighborhood children. He was chairman of the 1937 and 1938 parade committees, gathering more than 300 gifts for the children.[9]

Ray Schiller (far right) poses at the Parkside May Day celebration on May 7, 1944. Schiller's daughter Mary Lou is peeking out from behind the May Day Queen, Marilyn Crane. Schiller is surrounded by other members of the Parkside District Improvement Club.

Ray Schiller stood next to "conductor" Mayor Angelo Rossi (far right) on the first car of the L line extension on September 15, 1937. Also in the photo are Public Utilities Commission (PUC) president Lewis Byington and, next to him, PUC manager Edward Cahill.

Schiller's major concern was that the Parkside not be forgotten by city leaders. He said to one reporter in 1937, "Yes, sir, we've got a wonderful residential district out here, the fastest growing in the city—750 new homes in the last year. But nobody seems to realize it. We haven't even got a Supervisor from this section of San Francisco. We're not trying to elect one, but we do want a little attention from those already in office."[10]

The Parkside District Improvement Club began its most ambitious campaign in 1927. The club hoped to persuade the city to build a high school named after President Abraham Lincoln. Schiller jumped right into this campaign. "What we need most is that high school," he said. "About 3,000 children from our district right now have to pay two fares to get to the high schools they are compelled to attend, and the cars are so crowded they can't get on them."[11] The PDIC lobbied for support of an educational bond measure in 1938, and voters approved it. The school was dedicated on September 22, 1940. Schiller was a member of the school dedication committee.

STEPPING DOWN AS PRESIDENT

After three years as president of the PDIC, Schiller stepped down. He refused to be nominated for a fourth term, arguing that three terms were enough for any president. On January 13, 1940, the Parkside District Improvement Club gave a party to celebrate Schiller's work as president. "Friends came from all over the city, and he has a great many friends," wrote a reporter at the *San Francisco Chronicle*. "Ray is identified with practically any group you can mention."[12]

Ray Schiller displays the case he made for a Schilling Spices salesman.

Throughout the 1930s and 1940s Schiller held various leadership positions. He served on a grand jury in 1934. He was president of the Parkside Merchants Association in 1938 and was on the World's Fair Advisory Commission for the 1939 Golden Gate International Exposition. He was the local director of the National Association for Advancement of the Blind, a member of the Eagles Club, and a member of the San Francisco Russia War Relief Committee. He was also an honorary life member of the San Francisco Press Club (although he was not a journalist) and an honorary member of the Parkside Tennis Club (although he did not play tennis).

In a 1940 column he wrote for the *San Francisco Chronicle*, Schiller called the Parkside "[t]he district that knows how." He wrote,

> That's Parkside, the fastest growing part of town. Those hardy pioneers who came from the downtown section just after the turn of the century started the growth. Today Parkside is in the second largest voting district of San Francisco and boasts leaders in every phase of civic activity. … It's a great district, a cooperative one. When there is an improvement needed or when a threat appears the residents get together and bring about the result they desire.[13]

Ray Schiller appeared in many newspaper photographs and articles announcing Parkside events. He was always there and always seemed to be smiling—and whistling. Schiller could silence a crowd with his distinctive whistles, which sounded like fire engine and police sirens.

On Schiller's work to get services for the Parkside, one reporter wrote, "He is not a conniver, not a string puller nor a cheap politician. He expresses the honest wants of his community and the powers that be listen to him."[14]

"When I was a child, I remember that Governor Earl Warren had his driver stop by our house so that he could buy luggage for his wife. As he shopped, state troopers leaned against the car, and neighborhood children, suspecting the worst, asked me, 'What did you do?'"

—

Rita Schiller Aldrich,
Ray Schiller's daughter

"During the war, we'd be on Market Street with lots of sailors and Marines walking around. If one started to walk across the street against the light, my dad would do one of his police whistle imitations. Everyone would stop and look around."

—

Rita Schiller Aldrich

"My father burst into that loud whistle whenever he saw someone he knew or when he entered the San Francisco Press Club."

—

Mary Lou Schiller Blackfield,
Ray Schiller's daughter

"Mr. Schiller earned his title of 'Mayor of the Parkside' through his many years of energetic work on behalf of the Parkside residents. He led battles for schools, transit facilities and many other improvements for the district."

—

"Ray Schiller Dies at the Press Club,"
San Francisco Chronicle,
January 2, 1949

Schiller was attending a San Francisco Press Club New Year's Eve party when he collapsed shortly after midnight, just as the new year of 1949 was beginning. A heart attack had taken his life. He was fifty-three years old.

Obituaries ran in publications throughout the city. To the San Francisco Press Club, "Ray Schiller meant Saturday night dances, the warm hand of friendship, and continuing service."[15] The South of Market Boys wrote, "Ray's passing is mourned by his many friends throughout the city. ... We have lost a fine pal, true friend, and loyal worker and will long miss Ray's genial personality."

In the 1990s, the city built three boarding platforms on Taraval Street for the L streetcar. These platforms feature photos of Parkside residents. One photo shows Schiller's wife, Mary Louise, and daughter Rita, but there is no photo of Schiller. No Sunset street, park, or building is named after him; nothing tangible commemorates his short life and the work he did for his neighborhood. Schiller was an ordinary, unassuming man who exemplified the principle of giving back to his city by doing what he could to make it a better place to live. His legacy lives in his simple contributions to residents' quality of life, contributions that earned him the title "Mayor of the Parkside."

JOSEPHINE COLE: A PIONEER TEACHER (1913–2006)

Josephine Cole stood in the vanguard in many areas of her life. Now almost forgotten in San Francisco history, Josephine and her husband, Audley, achieved several professional firsts for African Americans in San Francisco. They also moved to the Sunset District at a time when most residents were Caucasian.

Josephine (Jo) Elizabeth Foreman was born on January 18, 1913, at 3335 Buchanan Street in San Francisco. She was named after her father, Joseph Foreman, and her mother, Elizabeth. An excellent student, she went to Jean Parker Elementary School, where she skipped a few grades and graduated when she was nine years old. After graduating from Girls' High School, she attended the University of California, Berkeley, where she majored in economics and was a member of the Phi Beta Kappa academic honorary society. She graduated at the age of eighteen and later earned a secondary teaching credential and a master's degree.

Josephine Cole

Josephine Cole Breaks Color Barriers

Josephine Cole knew as a child that she wanted to be a teacher, but African American teachers were not welcome in San Francisco schools in the mid-twentieth century. After earning her teaching credential, Cole applied to the San Francisco Unified School District (SFUSD). She later explained what happened.

> They used to have a seven-hour written examination, National Teachers' Examination. After you passed the written part, if you did, you had an oral interview. So when it came to my oral interview, I was given zero by the interviewers. That put me on the list, so they could avoid being called discriminating. But I was so far down on the list that the list expired before I ever got called. So, to keep my teaching credential alive, which you have to do, I started at St. Vincent's.[16]

In 1935, Cole began teaching French and American history at St. Vincent's, a girls' Catholic elementary school. In the early 1940s, she again leapt at a chance to work for SFUSD. "World War II came along and they needed teachers," she said. She took the examination again and, in 1944, became the first African American teacher hired by the district. She taught at Raphael Weill (now Rosa Parks) Elementary School.

Ultimately, Cole wanted to teach high school students, so she had to take yet another examination. After scoring second in history and third in English, she was assigned to teach English at Balboa High School in 1948. She was the first African American teacher in a San Francisco high school. She taught there until 1963.

> *"Josephine Cole was an elegant woman who spoke with candor and insight but also tact. She had a strong sense of right and wrong, but wasn't 'militant.' She loved her father, 'Joe Shreve,' who had the most visible position of any African American of his era, doorman/greeter for Shreve, a downtown jewelry store catering to the city's elite."*
>
> —
>
> Jesse Warr, interviewer of Josephine Foreman Cole in 1978

> *"We had a class [in our house]. I called it the English Lab because the kids ran it. We were selected as the People-to-People Outstanding Class in the nation."*
>
> —
>
> Josephine Foreman Cole, interview with Jesse Warr, 1978, p. 17

> *"Hooray! The library at City College's new southeast campus has been named for Josephine Cole, the city's first full-time black teacher, and it couldn't happen to a more deserving person—or family. Her husband, Audley, was the first black motorman hired by the Muni (in '42) and went through hell to achieve that distinction. Josephine is the daughter of an unforgettable San Franciscan— Joseph 'Joe Shreve' Foreman, the tall, slender, dignified doorman at Shreve's jewelry palace…"*
>
> —
>
> Columnist Herb Caen, *San Francisco Chronicle*, June 1993

Audley Cole in a photograph that appeared in the *People's World* on February 14, 1942.

After teaching at Balboa, Cole held a variety of positions, including educational counselor in the SFUSD Bayview–Hunters Point Youth Opportunities Project, guidance service centers director for SFUSD's Special Education Division, and supervisor of Student Relations and Community Committee. In June 1971 she chaperoned a student trip to Japan.

Cole also taught black literature at City College of San Francisco (CCSF) and was a part-time lecturer in urban problems at the University of San Francisco. After retiring in 1974, she worked as an education officer for the U.S. Department of State. She was named Educator of the Decade by the SFUSD in 1978 and was appointed a lifetime consultant to the district. In 1993 she received the San Francisco Mayor's Award for Leadership, and in 1995 the board of supervisors named her an Outstanding Community Leader of San Francisco. Cole also received awards from the National Council of Negro Women, Phi Lambda Theta sorority, and the San Francisco African American Historical and Cultural Society. In 1992, the library at CCSF's southeast campus was named the Josephine Cole Library.

"JOE SHREVE" AND AUDLEY COLE

Josephine's father, Joseph Foreman, had been a doorman at St. Dunstan's Hotel, which was destroyed in the 1906 earthquake and fire. After the owners of Shreve's rebuilt their jewelry store at Post and Grant, they hired him as a doorman. He held that position for more than forty-five years and became known as "Joe Shreve." Josephine once said that her father "brought dignity to that job in the days when it wasn't easy for a minority to find work."[17]

Josephine Foreman met Audley Cole in 1940; they married in 1941. The Coles had no children. During the first sixteen years of their marriage they lived in a small apartment on Bush Street.

Audley Cole is recognized for having broken the color barrier by becoming the first black motorman hired by the San Francisco Municipal Railway (Muni). This was not an easy task. In December 1941, Cole took and passed the civil service examination without noting his race. Muni hired him and assigned other motormen to train him.

At first, seventeen motormen agreed to train Cole, but one by one they refused. One who agreed to give the training "received a serious injury to the back of the head by an unknown assailant as he stood on the corner of Van Ness Avenue and Market Street."[18] The motormen's union threatened to levy a $100 fine against anyone who agreed to train Cole. (This threat was later rescinded.) The union threatened to strike if motormen were required to train and accept his hiring.

Fourteen motormen were suspended for refusing to provide training. (The union reimbursed them for the money they lost through the suspensions.) Mayor Rossi initially supported the suspensions, saying, "If the colored person is good enough to be a soldier, he is good enough to work for this city. The man passed his civil service examination, and should be able to work. We are not going to turn anyone down because of his race."[19] The mayor later supported a compromise offered to the motormen—that a senior member of the training department, instead of individual motormen, would give Cole his training. Cole joined the ranks of Muni as the first black motorman in March 1942.

THE COLES AND THE SUNSET

The Coles' ties to the Sunset District began when they bought a house at 1598 36th Avenue, which would be their home for fifty years. This house, originally designed and built by Oliver Rousseau for his family (see pages 58–9), became home to Audley and Josephine Cole in November 1957, at a time when few nonwhite people lived in the Sunset District. There is no public record of any difficulties with the neighbors, and neither Josephine nor Audley spoke publicly about problems living in the neighborhood.

The Sunset house became a gathering place for Josephine's students. "That's one of the reasons we bought the house," she said, "because I wanted to do things that I didn't want

"I have been more than a little upset by the Municipal Railway Carmen refusing to train a Negro in the job he is capable of filling as well as themselves. Such discrimination is particularly bad now when we are fighting a war to give equality to every man, regardless of color."

—

J. B. Milford, letter to the editor,
San Francisco Chronicle,
March 10, 1942, p. 14

"Cole is at last a full-fledged motorman in the service of the Municipal Railway. … Democracy has triumphed; Audley Cole has triumphed. … Today the grass is greener, the sky is bluer and the Stars and Stripes whip defiance in the breeze to all those, at home and abroad, who would mistreat the humblest American."

—

Isaaq N. Braan,
letter to the editor,
San Francisco Chronicle,
March 28, 1942, p. 12

"I remember when the Coles moved into the house. People in the neighborhood may have talked about it, but I don't recall any big concern about it. … I never met Josephine Cole. I remember that Mr. Cole was outside all the time watering the lawn. The outside was well maintained.

—

Frank O'Brien

to do in a school environment."[20] She frequently hosted student meetings and classes, including a Japanese language class after her retirement. For one series of classes, the Coles invited a variety of accomplished people—including actor Vincent Price and entertainer/actress Josephine Baker—to their home. They also hosted international teachers.

The Coles' house in the Sunset District.

Josephine Cole died on March 22, 2006. Her husband, Audley Cole, died on May 24, 2008. The Coles' Sunset home on 36th Avenue was sold in 2010, fifty-two years after they moved in.

A FEW OTHER NOTABLE SUNSET RESIDENTS

ACTING (ALL WITH PARTIAL LISTS OF APPEARANCES)

- **Joan Blackman** (movies: *Blue Hawaii, Visit to a Small Planet*; television: various programs, including *Peyton Place*)

- **Linda Bulgo** (movies: *Sister Act* and *Tales of the City*; local theater: *Beach Blanket Babylon*)

- **Barbara Eden** (Miss San Francisco, 1961; television: *I Dream of Jeannie*; various movies, including *Flaming Star*)

- **Laura June Kenny** (television: *The Little Rascals*) (author of the book *Fleeing the Fates of the Little Rascals*)

Barbara Eden

- **Jeffrey Tambor** (television: many programs, including *Barney Miller, Hill Street Blues, Arrested Development, The Larry Sanders Show*; movies: *And Justice for All, There's Something About Mary*).

Blackman and Eden, both graduates of Lincoln High School, also shared the experience of costarring in movies with Elvis Presley—Blackman in *Blue Hawaii* and Eden in *Flaming Star*.

MUSIC

Vince Guaraldi was born in San Francisco on July 17, 1928, and graduated from Lincoln High School in 1946. His jazz music became popular in the 1950s, but he is perhaps best known for composing the song "Cast Your Fate to the Wind" and writing and playing the music in various Peanuts television specials.

SPORTS

Mike Holmgren was born in San Francisco on June 15, 1948. He attended Abraham Lincoln High School, where he played football as tight end and then as quarterback. Later, he taught history and coached football at Lincoln and then coached football at Brigham Young University and other colleges. He began an illustrious professional football coaching career for the San Francisco 49ers. He has since worked as head coach for the Green Bay Packers and Seattle Seahawks and as president of the Cleveland Browns.

Fred Van Dyke was born on July 2, 1929, and lived in various Sunset houses until his parents were able to buy a Doelger house on 34th Avenue. He attended St. Anne's School through eighth grade and then graduated in 1946 "with a D average" from the new Lincoln High School. Van Dyke's memoir, *Once upon Abundance: Coming of Age in California and Hawaii*, describes growing up in the Sunset District and then moving to Hawaii. Over time, he became a legendary pioneer in the sport of riding the huge, 30-foot waves of Hawaii's coastline. He helped found and later wrote for *Surfer* magazine and was senior editor at *Ocean Sports International* magazine for six years. He appeared as a surfer in the 1960s Hollywood movies *Beach Blanket Bingo* and *Ride the Wild Surf* and was part of the 2001 video documentary *Surfing for Life*, which highlighted surfers in their 70s, 80s, and 90s. Van Dyke still writes and gives public presentations.

Fred Van Dyke

NEWSCASTING

Terry Lowry was born in Oakland. When she was a child, her family moved to 47th Avenue and Rivera Street in San Francisco. She attended Giannini Junior High School, Lincoln High School, and San Francisco State College. After teaching for a short time in San Francisco schools, she moved into broadcasting in 1970, translating the evening news into Spanish via simulcast. A twenty-five-year career on local television as a news and weather anchor/reporter and talk show host followed. Since 1980 Lowry and her broadcaster husband, Fred LaCosse, have owned their own business, LaCosse Productions, which produces corporate videos, conducts communication-training seminars, and offers talent services. Lowry has received multiple awards for her public service work and is active on various volunteer boards.

Terry Lowry

"A boy in my geometry class always asked me to show him my homework, saying he was too busy to complete his assignment every afternoon, playing golf with his dad, a 'pro' at a San Francisco course. My classmate was named Kenny Venturi, who later became a CBS sportscaster, and earlier, a winner of many golf tournaments."

—

Laura June Kenny,
Fleeing the Fates of the Little Rascals,
p. 124

"I met a wonderful person, Cliff Kamaka, at the beach in the 1940s. He taught me how to body-surf in the frigid Ocean Beach water. (Wet suits hadn't been invented yet!) It was fantastic to have such a wonderful outlet. It was so satisfying. There was nothing frustrating in it. If you wanted to swim out to the breakers, you could do it. If you wanted to catch a wave, you could do it. And there was no one out there. You were all by yourself (with probably a few white sharks)."

—

Fred Van Dyke

"There was nothing there. There were two black-top streets that had streetcars, Taraval and Judah. Other than that, there were just sand dunes. … I pretty much lived between the beach, the Golden Gate Park and the zoo. My perception was formed by the sea and the sand dunes." [21]

—

Richard Serra, when asked
what it was like growing up in
San Francisco's Sunset
District in the 1940s

POLITICS AND LAW

John Burton.

Phillip and **John Burton** were born in Cincinnati, Phillip in June 1926 and John in December 1932. In the summer of 1941, the family moved to Kirkham Street in San Francisco. Phillip graduated from George Washington High School, and John graduated from Abraham Lincoln High School. Phillip served in the U.S. House of Representatives from 1964 to 1983 and was known for helping to create the Golden Gate National Recreation Area. He died in April 1983. John Burton served in the California State Assembly from 1965 to 1974, was a U.S. congressman from 1975 to 1982, and again was a state assemblyman from 1988 to 1996. He was a state senator from 1996 to 2004, serving as president pro tem. After retiring from the California Senate, he founded the John Burton Foundation for Children without Homes in 2004.

Laurence H. Tribe was born in Shanghai in 1941 and later moved to San Francisco, where he attended Abraham Lincoln High School. He received an A.B. in mathematics from Harvard University and a J.D. from Harvard Law School, where he is now the Carl M. Loeb University Professor of Law. A respected scholars of Constitutional Law, Tribe has written many books and has argued before the U.S. Supreme Court more than thirty times.

Wendy Nelder graduated from Abraham Lincoln High School in 1958 and later from the University of California, Berkeley, and Hastings College of the Law. After practicing law in San Francisco and Washington, D.C., she became San Francisco's city attorney in the late 1970s. She was elected to the board of supervisors in 1980 and became its president in 1982. After three terms, Nelder left the board in 1991 and returned to private law practice.

ART

Sculptor **Richard Serra** was born in San Francisco in 1939 and attended San Francisco schools, graduating from Lincoln High School. He attended both University of California, Berkeley, and University of California, Santa Barbara, and graduated with a degree in English literature. While in Santa Barbara, he began working in steel mills to support himself. (He later graduated from Yale University with both a BFA and an MFA.) Serra's early work in the 1960s focused on the industrial materials—steel and lead—that he had worked with in steel mills and shipyards. Serra's work has become famous for its breathtaking size and weight. His public artwork includes the sixty-foot-tall "Charlie Brown," installed in San Francisco in 2000.

NOTES

1. Descriptions of these Easter parties appear in Stan Adair, *Spell Hippopotamus* (p. 58), and Mary Ada Williams with George Stanton, *More Parkside Pranks and Sunset Stunts* (pp. 74–75).

2. "Sales of Lots Assessed for Twin Peaks Tunnel," *San Francisco Chronicle,* May 24, 1914, p. 68.

3. "Supervisors to Dedicate New Park in Sunset Area," *San Francisco Chronicle,* September 27, 1926, p. 1.

4. "Donor of Playground Site Honored by Mayor, Officials," *San Francisco Chronicle,* October 5, 1926, p. 3.

5. "Larsen Given Eulogies by Supervisors," *San Francisco Chronicle,* November 6, 1928, p. 12.

6. "Larsen Heirs Face Contest for Estate," *San Francisco Chronicle,* September 28, 1929, p. 3.

7. "Larsen Will Invalid: City Out $500,000," *San Francisco Chronicle,* May 6, 1931, p. 8.

8. Marble's comments are from Alice Marble with Dale Leatherman, *Courting Danger,* pp. 3–4.

9. Parkside District Improvement Club (PDIC) Scrapbook, vol. 1, San Francisco History Center, San Francisco Public Library.

10. Neil Hitt, "He Gives His Awl for Progress, Gets Left Holding the Bag," *San Francisco Chronicle,* March 5, 1937, p. 19.

11. Ibid.

12. Bill Simons, "In the Neighborhoods," *San Francisco Chronicle,* January 14, 1940, p. 8.

13. Ray Schiller, "In the Districts: Churches, Industries, Parks, Parkside's Got Everything!" *San Francisco Chronicle,* September 2, 1940, p. 11.

14. Neil Hitt, "He Gives His Awl."

15. "Ray Schiller Dies at Club Fete for '49," *Black Kitten,* January 1949, p. 1.

16. Mildred Hamilton, "A Life-long Teacher Who's Still Eager to Learn Everything," *San Francisco Sunday Examiner and Chronicle,* August 8, 1982, p. 5.

17. Jesse Warr, interview with Josephine Foreman Cole, p. 61.

18. Richard Grant, *The Case of Audley Cole: Racial Policy in the AFL and the CIO,* unpublished paper, San Francisco State University, Fall 1993.

19. "Negro Case: Union Stands Firm in Street Car Dispute," *San Francisco Chronicle,* March 7, 1942, p. 9.

20. Jesse Warr, interview with Josephine Foreman Cole, p. 17.

21. Geoffrey A. Fowler, "Sculptor Revisits His Early Haunts," *Wall Street Journal,* October 20, 2011.

Zookeepers hold "new members" of the San Francisco Zoo in the 1930s.

CHAPTER 10

NOTABLE PLACES

The Sunset District hosts five buildings (and one sculptured dog head) that are registered City Landmarks. This chapter presents these landmarks and then describes other significant places that have been part of the Sunset's history.

LANDMARKS

10TH AVENUE FIREHOUSE

On December 8, 1898, the headline in the *San Francisco Call* newspaper exclaimed, "Joy in Sunset Valley: The Favored Section to be [P]rovided with Water and Fire Protection." The article announced that the board of supervisors planned to advertise for bids to build a firehouse at 1348 10th Avenue and had agreed to instruct the Spring Valley Water Co. "to run mains through all of the graded streets in the Sunset district of the city."

In 1899, Engine Company No. 22 (originally named Chemical Engine No. 2) opened in the two-story wood-frame building designed by Charles R. Wilson on 10th Avenue. In 1962, the firehouse moved to a new facility at 1290 16th Avenue. The 10th Avenue building was sold at public auction in 1969 and became Landmark No. 29 in 1970.

The first Registered City Landmark in the Sunset District: the firehouse on 10th Avenue.

EARTHQUAKE COTTAGE

After the 1906 earthquake and fire destroyed homes in San Francisco, thousands of people lived in tents for months, a hardship especially during the rainy winter season. A remarkable refugee relief project built 5,610 temporary residences in the form of one-room wooden houses called earthquake cottages. San Francisco established camps with these cottages on parkland around the city (none in the Sunset), and people paid about $2 per month to stay in a cottage.

In 1907 the city began a campaign to remove the cottages and reclaim the parks. People who moved cottages out of the camps received a refund of the monthly fee they had paid and could keep a cottage if they moved it off city parkland. The city got back its parks, and people could own inexpensive "starter homes." While the Sunset District never hosted an earthquake cottage camp, the neighborhood had empty lots to which many residents moved their earthquake cottages and established their new homes.

In 1906, Camp Richmond, an earthquake cottage camp, stood on what is now Park Presidio Boulevard in the Richmond District.

Landmark #171 sits at 1227 24th Avenue.

In 1982, Jane Cryan was renting a small house on 24th Avenue, which she learned was made up of three or four earthquake cottages. Cryan researched the house's history, founded the Society for the Preservation and Appreciation of San Francisco's 1906 Earthquake Refugee Shacks (no longer in operation), and shared what she had learned with city departments. In 1984, the City and County of San Francisco declared the house at 1227 24th Avenue City Landmark No. 171. The house still stands today, although the interior has been changed significantly.[1]

Eileen (Wassermann) Hershberg remembers that her family lived in a former earthquake cottage at 1729 24th Avenue (no longer standing), five blocks away from the cottages that were later landmarked. Only about twenty to thirty earthquake cottages have been discovered still standing in and around San Francisco

Eileen (Wassermann) Hershberg and her family lived in this earthquake cottage on 24th Avenue in the late 1950s.

In 2002, a local neighborhood group, the Western Neighborhoods Project (WNP), identified four earthquake cottages on Kirkham Street near 47th Avenue. The owners, who had planned to raze the cottages, changed their minds when they learned of their cottages' historical significance. Thanks to the efforts of volunteers and an offer of land for storage from the San Francisco Zoological Gardens, the WNP was able to save the buildings. Volunteers restored one cottage to its original state and put it on display on Market Street for the earthquake centenary in 2006. This cottage remains on display at the zoo. The WNP received the 2007 Governor's Historic Preservation Award for this work.[2]

In 2002, the Western Neighborhoods Project saved an earthquake cottage like the one on the left from destruction and restored it to its original state and color (right).

The original Shriners Hospital on 19th Avenue.

SHRINERS HOSPITAL FOR CRIPPLED CHILDREN

The Shriners, a "fraternity based on fun, fellowship and the Masonic principles of brotherly love, relief and truth," first became known in San Francisco when the group contributed $25,000 to help the city rebuild after the 1906 earthquake. In the 1920s, the Shriners began building children's hospitals around the country, beginning in Shreveport, Louisiana. San Francisco's Shriners Hospital for Crippled Children (the word *Crippled* was later dropped) was built in 1923 at 1651 19th Avenue. The hospital closed in 1997, relocating to Sacramento.

When the land was sold to a developer, preservationists feared that townhouses and condominiums would soon cover the entire site, but in a happy compromise, the City of San Francisco declared the original Shriners Hospital building Landmark No. 221 in 1998, while the rest of the land, on which additional hospital buildings had been constructed, was made available for development. The original building remains, serving as a nursing home. The other buildings were razed for new townhouses built in the early 2000s.

SUNSET BRANCH LIBRARY

Andrew Carnegie (1835–1919) and the Carnegie Corporation provided funding for more than 2,500 public library buildings around the world. In San Francisco, eight libraries were built using Carnegie funds: the old Main Library (now the Asian Art Museum), as well as the Chinatown, Mission, Golden Gate Valley, Noe Valley, Presidio, Richmond, and Sunset branch libraries.

The Sunset branch of the San Francisco Public Library, the fifth Carnegie library built in San Francisco, opened on March 25, 1918. According to the library's website, its location at

Sunset Branch Library on 18th Avenue.

1305 18th Avenue "was formerly the site of an old barn, which had become quite a nuisance in the neighborhood because young boys used it for gun practice." Designed by architect G. Albert Lansburgh, the two-story library cost $43,955 to build. It was declared Landmark No. 239 in 2004.

INFANT SHELTER

The Infant Shelter/Conservatory of Music/Lycée Français La Pérouse at 19th Avenue and Ortega Street.

The building at 1201 Ortega Street, at 19th Avenue, was constructed as the Infant Shelter in 1928–29 and served as an orphanage until 1956, when it became the San Francisco Conservatory of Music. In the early 2000s, the Conservatory of Music announced plans to build a new home in the city's Civic Center area. In 2004, San Francisco declared the original building Landmark No. 242; the Conservatory of Music moved out in 2006. Since 2007, the buildings have housed middle school and high school classes of Lycée Français La Pérouse, a French school.

DOGGIE DINER HEAD

Before McDonald's and other well-known fast food restaurants, the Doggie Diner, founded by Al Ross, was a popular Bay Area fixture. At one time, twenty-six Doggie Diner "drive-in restaurants" served hot dogs, burgers, and chili in the Bay Area. Thirteen of them were located in San Francisco. The chain's signature image was a red dachshund head designed in 1960 by Harold Bachman.

One of the last remaining Doggie Diner buildings in San Francisco stood at 2765 Sloat Boulevard. (Its name was later changed to Carousel.) In the early 2000s, the owners of the property wanted to remove all vestiges of the now-defunct Doggie Diner. Citizens lobbied to save the building and the signature dachshund head. The City of San Francisco moved the dog head to the center of Sloat Boulevard in 2005 and, in 2006, declared the head Landmark No. 254.

An original Doggie Diner on Sloat Boulevard.

OTHER NOTABLE PLACES IN THE SUNSET

EDGEWOOD CENTER

Edgewood Center was founded in 1851 as the San Francisco Orphan Society, a shelter for orphans of the California Gold Rush. Its home for many years was on Haight Street between Buchanan and Laguna. After the building was damaged in the 1906 earthquake, the organization's leaders sought a

Edgewood Center on Vicente Street between 30th and 31st Avenue.

new site, purchased ten acres at 1801 Vicente Street, and opened a new facility in 1924. Now called the Edgewood Center for Children and Families, the organization serves hundreds of abused and neglected children in San Mateo and San Francisco Counties through residential, community, and school-based programs.

PINEHURST LODGE

Not far from Edgewood is the distinctive brick building known as Pinehurst Lodge, at 2685 30th Avenue. Built by the Junior League of San Francisco, the facility opened in 1929 as Pinehaven, the Junior League Home for Homeless Children. Pinehaven provided a refuge for children waiting for placement in foster homes.

For its work designing Pinehaven, the architectural firm Ashley, Evers & Hayes received a 1929 "city clubhouses" award. The exterior was originally painted white, and the interior featured images designed to appeal to children: tiles of animals, ships, and castles decorate the walls of the recreation room, and a frieze of Old King Cole appears above the fireplace in the visitors' room.

Pinehurst Lodge on 30th Avenue.

The salon at the front of the building was donated by the Ghirardelli family in memory of their daughter Esperance. The ceiling of the salon displays Latin inscriptions with text from Corinthians 1:13: "So faith, hope, love remain, these three; but the greatest of these is love."

In 1939, the Junior League gave Pinehaven to the San Francisco Nursery for Homeless Children, which provided temporary homes for children five to twelve years of age. After purchasing the facility in 1946, the Salvation Army removed the white paint, exposing the brick construction, and renamed the facility Pinehurst Lodge. It currently operates as the Salvation Army's Women's Residence, a residential drug rehabilitation facility.

THE LITTLE SHAMROCK

The Little Shamrock traces its roots to the building of the 1894 California Midwinter Fair in Golden Gate Park. As the fairgrounds were being built in 1893, Antoine Herzo and his wife founded the Little Shamrock, an Irish pub, less than a mile away on H Street (now Lincoln Way), just outside the 9th Avenue entrance to the park. The builders of the fair went to the Little Shamrock for lunch and a schooner of beer. Mr. Herzo died around the time the pub began, and his widow

The Little Shamrock circa 1900.

continued the business with her new husband, J. P. Quigley. The pub has stood in the same location since its founding and is probably the oldest continuously running business in the Sunset. According to the Little Shamrock, "Times were difficult during the Prohibition years but there were many speakeasys throughout the city. Many of these went under the guise of cigar stores or harmless eating establishments."

OCEAN PARK MOTEL

On April 30, 1937, San Francisco's first motel opened. The Streamline Moderne Ocean Park Motor Court (now called the Ocean Park Motel), at 2690 46th Avenue, was designed by Conrad Kett with a distinctive nautical theme. The original owner, C. L. (Larry) Smith, must have anticipated the widespread use of the automobile; although few people in the Sunset owned cars in the 1930s, the Ocean Park Motel features parking spaces for customers.

The Little Shamrock today.

An early Ocean Park Motor Court postcard.

When it opened, the motel was surrounded by sand dunes and had an unobstructed view of the ocean. Now it is surrounded by a quiet residential neighborhood. The 1937 extension of the L Taraval streetcar line changed the route, and the streetcar now stops in front of the motel.

In 1987 the San Francisco Art Deco Society gave the current owners, Marc and Vicki Duffett, an award for preserving "[t]he first motel in San Francisco, opening 20 April 1937, in the Sunset District in time for the fiesta opening of the Golden Gate Bridge."

> *"When my grandparents moved to San Francisco, St. Anne's masses were held in the house of the pastor's cousin, a block from the church. The stained glass windows at the original St. Anne's were in memory of my grandparents, Thomas and Mary Faulkner. The stained glass window is still in the new church. It shows St. Anne in a brown/orange cloak. It's in a side altar, second window from the altar."*
>
> —
>
> Catherine Murphy (born 1914)

St. Anne of the Sunset Catholic Church

When St. Anne parish was founded in 1904, it had no church building. The parishioners held mass inside a meeting hall at 9th Avenue and H Street (now Lincoln Way). The first St. Anne of the Sunset Church was built in 1905 at the corner of Irving and 13th Avenue (now Funston). It was damaged in the 1906

St. Anne of the Sunset Catholic Church at 850 Judah Street.

Sister Justina, a Dominican nun, designed and created the frieze at St. Anne's.

earthquake, but it remained in use until the new church was built at Judah and Funston in the 1930s. In the early days, St. Anne's was the only Catholic church serving the entire Sunset District. Five Catholic churches now serve the area.

Perhaps the most noticeable feature of St. Anne's Church is the detailed frieze above the doors to the entrance on Judah Street, conceived, designed, and created by Sister Justina, a Dominican nun who lived at Mission San Jose in Fremont. According to church records, Sister Justina was born Justina Niemierski on December 9, 1879, in East Prussia and "from early childhood displayed remarkable talent for drawing and modeling." She attended the Academy of Fine Arts in Berlin and, after graduation, won several prizes for her work. Instead of becoming an artist, she entered the Dominican novitiate in Germany in 1909 and later was assigned to Mission San Jose in Fremont, California. Recognized as a talented sculptor, Sister Justina was invited by the San Francisco Archdiocese to create the frieze for the new church.

HENRY DOELGER'S HEADQUARTERS

The building that housed Henry Doelger's sales and work office still stands at 320 Judah Street.

In the 1930s, Henry Doelger (see chapter 5) was on his way to being the most successful builder in the Sunset District. His office was operating out of a small garage near 8th Avenue and Judah Street when he asked Charles O. Clausen, one of his principal designers, to design a building for his

Henry Doelger's headquarters at 320 Judah Street.

growing company. The tall structure at 320 Judah was built in 1932 and contained both the sales force and the workrooms. The left portion of the building was added in 1940. Doelger's company was housed in this building until 1950 or 1951.

Ed Hageman worked as a draftsman for Doelger at 320 Judah. Many years later he drew rough floor plans of the building (see illustrations below) and explained:

> Henry Doelger's office ["H room"] was on the main floor, to the left as you went in. The lobby had a big receptionist desk in front, two desks behind, and two along the wall. To the right was the salesmen's area; to the left was Alpha Porter's desk. She was Henry Doelger's right hand and the bookkeeper. Boy oh boy. She ran the office.
>
> Upstairs, right above Henry's office, there was this big conference room ["CON"]. John Doelger's office was up there. There was also a bar with a kind of a Mexican motif—leather seats and all that. The big warehouse was in the back. All the hardware was back there—lock sets, storage, hardware.[3]

The building at 320 Judah featured a swinging door with a window. From the inside, one could see the Henry Doelger Builder logo (above), designed by Ed Hageman, one of his draftsmen. The door has been removed, but the window remains. The logo was used in many of Doelger's newspaper ads (below).

FIRST FLOOR

SECOND FLOOR

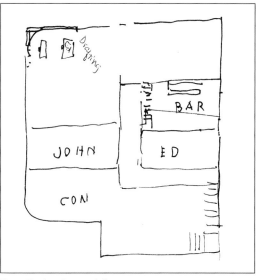

Ed Hageman drew these floor plans of 320 Judah and explained how Henry Doelger Inc. used the rooms.

Sigmund Stern Grove and Pine Lake Park

Sixty-three acres north of Sloat Boulevard from 19th to 34th Avenue comprise Sigmund Stern Grove and Pine Lake Park. This park refuge would not exist were it not for the Green (sometimes spelled Greene) family and civic leader Rosalie Stern, who bought the property and donated it to the City of San Francisco.

Pine Lake in the early days with cows on the shore.

Members of the Green family came to San Francisco from Maine in 1847 and settled "outside San Francisco," in the gully below what is now 19th Avenue and Sloat Boulevard. The family began farming and at one point was harvesting oats, barley, potatoes, and turnips on land extending two miles to the beach. In the 1870s George Green began planting the many eucalyptus and redwood trees that still stand on the property.

The Green homestead had a history of conflict. In 1876, landowner David Mahoney tried to take the land from the Greens. Owner of a land grant for the Rancho Laguna de la Merced, Mahoney filed a lawsuit claiming that his rancho extended northward to include the land the Greens called their own. When the U.S. Supreme Court ruled in Mahoney's favor, federal marshals arrived to evict the Greens, who refused to leave. Mrs. Green "barricaded the house and threatened to spill a vat of scalding water on the men if they ventured near."[4] As their lawyer appealed the case to Congress, the Greens built a metal-lined fort and a fence laced with dynamite to keep out the authorities. The standoff lasted for three months. In 1887, a special act of Congress awarded to the family the land from 19th Avenue to west of Pine Lake.

In 1892 George Green built the Trocadero Inn, a Victorian-style roadhouse that attracted the Bay Area elite and still stands today. Visitors in the 1890s enjoyed "a deer park, and a boating pavilion, and a beer garden, and the

This postcard promoted the Trocadero Inn, which George W. Green built in 1892.

finest trout farm in California."[5] Other attractions included dancing and overnight stays in cabins. Although it initially considered a high-quality establishment (an early ad advertised the Trocadero as "AN IDEAL FAMILY RESORT ... Meals Served at All Hours"), the Trocadero lost its good reputation over the years. According to an article in the San Francisco Performing Arts publication *Encore* (Spring 1987), "the Trocadero was innocent, the Trocadero was rowdy." Small holes in the front door are said to be bullet holes from various violent encounters, although no one seems to know the specifics.

Some people claim that the holes in the Trocadero's front door are bullet holes.

In 1907 San Francisco government officials, including the mayor and members of the board of supervisors, were prosecuted for alleged corruption and widespread graft. Most of these defendants had been controlled by attorney Abe Ruef, known as "Boss Ruef." He missed a court date and hid out at the Trocadero until the police found and arrested him. Some sources say there was a shootout, but most accounts indicate that Ruef went quietly with the police.

In 1916, George Green closed the Trocadero Inn and made it his home. Real estate maps show that developers hoped to fill in the Green property and build homes and

"It was young George [Green] who, in 1871, convinced the family to let him plant eucalyptus trees. Later he planted the Holland grass with its twenty-foot root system to keep the sand from drifting. Within a decade, they had forty-two planted acres on their land."

—

Jerry Fristo

"I had a dozen offers for the place. But I never sold—I knew they'd cut down the trees and tear down the inn, and I didn't want to see the work of sixty years go by the board. I planted the grove myself, you know, in '72—no, '73. But now the place is in good hands, and I guess that all the shooting and the fighting was worth while."

—

George Green, quoted in the *San Francisco Chronicle*, June 5, 1932, p. 8

streets like those that stand elsewhere in the Sunset. However, the Greens never sold the land to developers.

In 1931, Rosalie Stern bought twelve acres of this land from George Green and donated it to the city for a park to be named in honor of her late husband, Sigmund. The dedication was held on June 4, 1932. She hired famed architect Bernard Maybeck, known for designing the Palace of Fine Arts for the Panama Pacific Exposition in 1915, to restore the Trocadero. Stern also hired architect William Gladstone Merchant to help turn the wild lands into meadows and walking paths for visitors. When the new park was dedicated, a newspaper article thanked Rosalie Stern and Bernard Maybeck, adding, "But we hope that San Francisco will allow some measure of gratitude to old George Greene, who is neither wise nor delightful, but a bit bleary-eyed out at the elbows, and fond of strong language. It was he, remember, whose hand seeded the valley and who preserved it with rifle, lawsuit and dynamite for its present fate."[6]

Free summer concerts began in 1938 and continue today. The City of San Francisco later bought more land; now Sigmund Stern Grove and Pine Lake Park comprise sixty-three acres.

FLEISHHACKER DESTINATIONS

Herbert Fleishhacker was president of the San Francisco Park Commission when it bought land in the southwest area of San Francisco, just south of Sloat Boulevard. Within a few years, a pool, a playground, and a zoo—all carrying the Fleishhacker name—opened to the public. While not "technically" in the Sunset District, these destinations were close, convenient locations for recreation and entertainment for thousands of Sunset residents, as well as for other San Franciscans and visitors.

Fleishhacker Pool in 1960.

Fleishhacker Pool

Fleishhacker Pool opened in April 1925 in the southwest corner of San Francisco, next to the land that within a short time became the city's zoo. The pool was a popular swimming spot for almost fifty years. At 1,000 feet long and 100 feet at its widest point, it was the largest outdoor pool in the country when it opened. It was so large that lifeguards patrolled in rowboats. The pool held six million gallons of salt water pumped in from the Pacific Ocean, a few hundred yards away.

Fleishhacker Pool was so large that lifeguards patrolled in rowboats.

Although the city claimed that Fleishhacker Pool had a heating system, no one seems to remember the water being anything but cold. Famous competitive swimmers, including Ann Curtis and Buster Crabbe, swam at Fleishhacker. Charlie Sava gave swimming lessons at Fleishhacker, and Johnny Weissmuller set a world record there in the 100-yard freestyle.

Jack Goldsworthy met Ann Curtis, the Olympic swimmer, at Fleishhacker Pool. He remembered, "We used to swim the length of the pool. At one point, she said, 'Jack, this is too cold for me. You've got the Pacific Ocean, and the fog … I'm going to go to Marin County and open a swim club.' She went to San Rafael and opened a club to teach people how to swim."

"There were a few times it got so warm in San Francisco that school was discontinued for one or two days. We'd go down to Fleishhacker's and sneak in the pool. We got in and got out fast, before anyone caught us."

—

Andy Casper

"We didn't go in the pool very often because we didn't have the money. But my mother used to sew a lot. At Fleishhacker, the lifeguard always knew if everyone had paid because you were assigned a ribbon to put on your strap. Every day had a different color. We'd look around and see what color they were wearing that day. 'Oh, they're wearing red today,' so we'd put on red bias tape. No one knew the difference."

—

Frances Larkin

"Fleishhacker Pool was so large and so cold that mostly you didn't use it. I think that was the tragedy of Fleishhacker: you would go out there on a nice day, and the fog would come in. Another problem was that fish sometimes came in with the seawater."

—

Valerie Meehan

"Fleishhacker Pool wasn't that cold. When you got out of the water it was cold."

—

Jack Goldsworthy

Fleishhacker Pool was open every summer from 1925 to July 1971, except for a short period during World War II. However, by 1964, attendance and revenue had dropped sharply. Pool expenses for summer 1964 were $60,500, while only $7,000 in revenue was received.[7] The pool's decline has been attributed to the increased use of the automobile, which allowed people to travel farther for recreation; the cold weather in western San Francisco; and the increase in the number of neighborhood indoor pools. A storm in January 1971 damaged the intake/outfall pipe, and the Health Department closed the pool in July. A bond measure in 1977 would have restored the pool. The measure failed, and the pool never reopened. The huge hole that was Fleishhacker Pool has been filled in; the zoo's parking lot sits on top of the site.

Taken after Fleishhacker Pool was closed and drained, this photo shows the Bath House, which still stands, just west of the pool site.

Fleishhacker Pool Bath House

The Mediterranean-style bath house was designed in 1923–25 by Ward and Blohme, a San Francisco architecture company. The building is 450 feet long and originally featured more than twenty skylights that illuminated the ground floor. "Inside were lockers and changing rooms for up to 800 swimmers, ocean-facing dining rooms on the top floor, and a mini-hospital to care for slips and falls."[8]

The bath house was also used for public classes and workshops and by the Recreation Center for the Handicapped (now Janet Pomeroy Center) in the 1950s to the 1970s. It was closed in the 1970s, and ownership was transferred to the San Francisco Zoological Gardens in 1999. The bath house has become a haven for the homeless and has been deteriorating for many years, but the City of San Francisco has placed the building on its working list for possible landmark status.

The Zoo

The Herbert Fleishhacker Zoo (renamed the San Francisco Zoological Gardens in 1941) opened in 1929 beside Fleishhacker Pool and the children's playground. Some animals were moved to the site from Golden Gate Park, and Herbert Fleishhacker and others donated animals and exhibits over the years. Until May 15, 1970, entrance to the zoo was free.

In 1935, Fleishhacker worked with architect Lewis P. Hobart to design and build the major portion of the zoo through the federal government's Works Progress Administration (WPA). According to the San Francisco Zoo website, the $3.5 million project built the Elephant House, Lion House, Monkey Island, Sea Lions Exhibit, and Bear Grottos.

Lewis P. Hobart designed and WPA workers built exhibits, including the "Lions Yard" in this location at the San Francisco Zoo.

In the 1930s, President Franklin D. Roosevelt's Works Progress Administration (WPA) provided funding to build many exhibits in Fleishhacker Zoo. In the 1937 photo above, three men discuss construction underway near the zoo's new main fountain (upper left) and stairway (upper center). Today the area is fully landscaped. Lion statues sit on either side of the stairway, and the fountain is called the Lion Fountain.

"We lived on Lincoln Way. When there was a southern breeze, we could hear the zoo train whistle. Also, before the zoo built the lion's houses, the lions were out in the open, and they knew the food was coming. At five o'clock every day, the lions would roar. We could hear their roar if the wind was blowing."

—

Frances Larkin (born 1925)

"I got so used to these things that I felt good about them, and I'd wonder what was happening when I didn't hear the surf breaking at night, or the African lions and elephants at the zoo. It was perfectly natural to me. Fleishhacker Zoo was a long way away—I lived at 34th and Quintara—but the sound picked up."

—

Fred Van Dyke

The Children's Playground

The children's playground (then called the Herbert Fleishhacker Playfield) opened east of Fleishhacker Pool on April 30, 1925. Originally larger than it is today, the playfield held a wading pool for children, playground equipment, and two nonoperating vehicles: a train engine car and a cable car. For many years, children climbed on and around these stationary vehicles.

Children climbed over and through this train engine car that was parked in the zoo's Children's Playground.

Jane Hudson and her brother played in the large wading pool that used to be in the children's playground.

The Mothers Building

When Delia Fleishhacker died in 1925, her sons Herbert and Mortimer Fleishhacker honored her by building the Delia Fleishhacker Memorial Building, best known as the Mothers Building. Located next to the zoo playground, the Mothers Building was a place where mothers could relax and care for their young children. (According to a form nominating the building to the National Register of Historic Places, "Boys over the age of six were specifically excluded.") The building contained comfortable chairs, a small kitchen, and restrooms; at one time, tea and picnic lunches were provided to the women using the building.

The Mothers Building was designed by San Francisco architect George W. Kelham. At a time when most hired artists were men, the Mothers Building featured mosaics and murals created by

The Mothers Building was a gift from Herbert and Mortimer Fleishhacker in honor of their mother.

Mothers of small children could rest and enjoy tea in the Mothers Building.

The mosaics outside the Mothers Building were designed by Helen Bruton.

respected women artists. The exterior mosaics were designed by Helen Bruton and created by her and her two sisters, Margaret and Esther. The striking murals inside were painted by Helen K. Forbes and Dorothy W. Pucinelli.

At one time the Mothers Building housed the zoo gift shop, but it has been closed for many years. The City of San Francisco is considering landmark status for the building.

WEST SIDE DESTINATIONS

The popular destinations on the west side of San Francisco charged no admission fee for many years. Free venues included the zoo and children's playground, as well as Golden Gate Park's de Young Museum, Japanese Tea Garden, California Academy of Sciences, and Arboretum. During the summer, visitors enjoyed music, dancing, and other cultural events at free concerts in Sigmund Stern Grove. In the nearby Richmond District, Sutro Baths and Playland-at-the-Beach provided endless hours of low-cost fun for children and families from the Sunset and elsewhere. Some of these destinations—including Fleishhacker Pool, Sutro Baths, and Playland—no longer exist. The summer series in Sigmund Stern Grove is the only remaining activity that still charges no admission fee.

NOTES

1. Learn more about Jane Cryan's experiences with her earthquake cottage online at http://www.outsidelands.org/red_shacks.php.

2. For more information on and photos of the earthquake cottages, see the Western Neighborhoods Project website, www.outsidelands.org (search for "shacks").

3. Ed Hageman interview, October 26, 2006.

4. George and Emilia Hodel, "Old Trocadero Rancho Made Playground," *San Francisco Chronicle,* June 5, 1932, p. 7.

5. George Green quoted in George and Emilia Hodel, "Old Trocadero Rancho Made Playground," *San Francisco Chronicle*, p. 8, June 5, 1932.

6. Ibid.

7. Charles Hall, *Report #1: Documentation of Historic, Cultural and Architectural Importance of the Fleishhacker Pool*, p. 8.

8. Woody LaBounty, "Streetwise: Six Million Gallons," http://www.outsidelands.org/sw8.php.

CONCLUSION

Only a century ago, the foggy sand dunes west of Twin Peaks, sloping to the shores of the Pacific Ocean, were referred to as the Outside Lands, considered uninhabitable. Within decades, pioneer builders, residents, and community activists had transformed approximately 10 percent of the city into the Sunset District, a thriving neighborhood of affordable homes within the boundaries of the City of San Francisco.

The story of the transformation of the Sunset District was lived and documented by city leaders who fought to ensure that the Outside Lands would belong to the City of San Francisco; by pioneers who set up homesteads in this sandy "wilderness"; by builders who erected houses and businesses to build neighborhoods; by pioneer families eager to fulfill the American Dream of home ownership; and by community activists and leaders who worked to create and maintain a thriving, livable neighborhood.

What began as a development dominated by white, working-class families has become an ethnically and racially diverse area with a rich history of immigration and emigration, of struggle and achievement, of civility and eccentricity.

The evolution continues.

BIBLIOGRAPHY

Adair, Stan. *Spell Hippopotamus: A humorous look at growing up in San Francisco in the early 1920's.* Unpublished manuscript, undated.

Aguado, Steve. *Sunset Memories.* Unpublished manuscript, 1993.

"All Persons Born or Naturalized … The Legacy of *US v Wong Kim Ark,*" UC Hastings College of the Law Library, Summer 2001, http://library.uchastings.edu/library/topical-and-course-research-guides/wkadisplay/laws3.htm.

"Almost History: Mr. Levitt of the Sunset: Henry Doelger Built Homes and Homes and Homes," *San Francisco Magazine,* June 1990.

America's Fastest Selling Homes Are Built by Doelger (brochure), date unknown. Courtesy of the Prelinger Library, San Francisco.

Ancestry.com. California and Californians, vol. 3 (online database). Provo, UT: The Generations Network, Inc., 1998. Original data: Hunt, Rockwell D., ed. *California and Californians*, vol. III. Chicago: Lewis Publishing, 1932.

Atherton, Gertrude. *My San Francisco: A Wayward Biography.* Indianapolis, IN, and New York: Bobbs-Merrill Company, 1946.

Baxter, Josephine (Fearon). "1906 San Francisco Earthquake Copy of Letter to her Parents in Omaha, Nebraska Covering Period Tuesday, April 17 to Monday, April 23." Available from the Bancroft Library, University of California, Berkeley.

Bean, Walton. *Boss Ruef's San Francisco.* Berkeley: University of California Press, 1972.

Bradford, Calvin. "Financing Home Ownership: The Federal Role in Neighborhood Decline," *Urban Affairs Quarterly*, March 1979, 313–35.

Brandi, Richard. *San Francisco's West Portal Neighborhoods.* Charleston, SC: Arcadia Publishing, 2005.

Brandi, Richard, and Woody LaBounty. *San Francisco's Parkside District: 1905–1957: A Historical Context Statement.* Produced for the San Francisco Mayor's Office of Economic and Workforce Development, http://www.outsidelands.org/parkside-statement.pdf, March 2008.

Brown, Willie. "Mayor Willie Brown Reminisces." National Museum of African American History and Culture, http://nmaahc.si.edu/memory/view/19.

Chandler, Samuel C. *Gateway to the Peninsula: Official History of Daly City, California.* City of Daly City, 1973.

Clary, Raymond. *The Making of Golden Gate Park, The Early Years: 1865–1906.* San Francisco: Don't Call It Frisco Press, 1984.

Council for Civic Unity of San Francisco. *San Francisco's Housing Market—Open or Closed?* Undated report received by San Francisco Public Library, November 11, 1960.

Cox, Lynn D. *Alice Marble: More than a Tennis Player.* Master's thesis, California State University, Pomona, 1982.

Crouchett, Lawrence P. *William Byron Rumford.* El Cerrito, CA: Downey Place Publishing House, 1984.

Davidson, Sue. *Changing the Game: The Stories of Tennis Champions Alice Marble and Althea Gibson.* Seattle: Seal Press, 1997.

Draper, Joan E. *Edward H. Bennett: Architect and City Planner, 1874–1954.* Chicago: The Art Institute of Chicago, 1982.

Dwinelle, John W. *Colonial History [of the] City of San Francisco.* San Francisco: Towne & Bacon, Book and Job Printers, 1867. Reprinted 1978, Ross Valley Book Co.

Eichenberg, Timothy. *Housing in the Sunset: A Community in Transition.* Sunset-Parkside Education & Action Committee (SPEAK), 1974.

Elinson, Elaine, and Stan Yogi. *Wherever There's a Fight: How Runaway Slaves, Suffragists, Immigrants, Strikers, and Poets Shaped Civil Liberties in California.* Berkeley: Heyday Books, 2009.

Encore (publication of San Francisco Performing Arts), Spring 1987.

Field, Stephen J. *California Alcalde.* Oakland, CA: Biobooks, 1950.

Fimrite, Ronald. *The Olympic Club of San Francisco, 1860–2009.* San Francisco: The Olympic Club, 2010.

Fritz, Christian G. *Federal Justice in California: The California Court of Ogden Hoffman, 1851–1891.* Lincoln: University of Nebraska Press, 1991.

Gilliam, Harold. *The Face of San Francisco.* Garden City, NY: Doubleday, 1960.

——. *The San Francisco Experience.* Garden City, NY: Doubleday, 1972.

Golding, Val. *SAN FRANCISCO: that was THE CITY that was.* http://www.cable-car-guy.com/html/ccvalgolding.html, 2002.

Green, Alfred. *Life and Adventures of a 47-er of California.* Unpublished oral history, 1878. The Bancroft Library, University of California, Berkeley.

Hall, Charles. *Report #1: Documentation of Historic, Cultural and Architectural Importance of the Fleishhacker Pool.* Page & Associates, Inc., August 15, 1977.

Hansen, Gladys, and Emmet Condon. *Denial of Disaster: The Untold Story and Photographs of the San Francisco Earthquake and Fire of 1906.* San Francisco: Cameron & Company, 1990.

Hays, R. Allen. *The Federal Government and Urban Housing: Ideology and Change in Public Policy.* Albany, NY: State University of New York Press, 1985.

James, Marquis, and Bessie Rowland James. *A Biography of a Bank: The Story of Bank of America.* New York: Harper & Bros., 1954.

Kahn, Judd. *Imperial San Francisco.* Lincoln, NE: University of Nebraska Press, 1979.

Keil, Rob. *Little Boxes: The Architecture of a Classic Midcentury Suburb.* Daly City, CA: Advection Media, 2006.

Kenny, Laura June. *Fleeing the Fates of the Little Rascals.* Bloomington, IN: AuthorHouse, 2004.

LaBounty, Woody. *Carville-by-the-Sea: San Francisco's Streetcar Suburb.* San Francisco: Outside Lands Media, 2009.

Loeb, Carolyn. *Entrepreneurial Vernacular: Developers' Subdivisions in the 1930s.* Baltimore and London: Johns Hopkins University Press, 2001.

Marble, Alice, with Dale Leatherman. *Courting Danger.* New York: St. Martin's Press, 1991.

———. *The Road to Wimbledon.* New York: Charles Scribner's Sons, 1946.

Massey, Douglas, and Nancy A. Denton. *American Apartheid: Segregation and the Making of the Underclass.* Cambridge, MA: Harvard University Press, 1993.

McCunn, Ruthanne Lum. *An Illustrated History of the Chinese in America.* San Francisco: Design Enterprises of San Francisco, 1979.

———. *Chinese American Portraits: Personal Histories, 1828–1988.* San Francisco: Chronicle Books, 1988.

Miller, Paul T. *The Postwar Struggle for Civil Rights: African Americans in San Francisco, 1945–1975.* New York and London: Routledge, Taylor & Francis Group, 2010.

Mullen, Kevin. *The Toughest Gang in Town: Police Stories from Old San Francisco.* Novato, CA: Noir Publications, 2005.

Mulvany, James L. *Poppy, Our Father: Memories of a Man and His Family.* Unpublished manuscript, 1996.

Nee, Victor G., and Brett de Bary Nee. *Longtime Californ': A Documentary Study of an American Chinatown.* First Sentry Printing, 1973; reprinted Stanford: Stanford University Press, 1986.

O'Brien, Robert. *This Is San Francisco.* New York: Whittlesey House (McGraw-Hill), 1948.

O'Day, Edward F., ed. *Report on a Plan for San Francisco by Daniel H. Burnham.* San Francisco: Sunset Press, 1905.

Page, Charles Hall and Associates Inc. *Report #1: Documentation of Historic, Cultural and Architectural Importance of the Fleishhacker Pool,* August 15, 1977 (Available at San Francisco History Center, San Francisco Public Library).

Parkside District Improvement Club (PDIC) Scrapbook, vol. 1, San Francisco History Center, San Francisco Public Library.

Property deed for 1901 29th Avenue, notarized January 3, 1940, and registered with the City and County of San Francisco on January 7, 1940. Courtesy of Joyce Bauer and Ken Englund.

Robbins, Millie. *Tales of Love and Hate in Old San Francisco.* San Francisco: Chronicle Books, 1971.

San Francisco Block Book, 1910.

San Francisco City Directory, 1904, 1905, 1920s, 1930s.

San Francisco Municipal Reports, 1859–60, 1862–63, 1863–64, 1865–66.

Schaffer, Hazel Drescher. "Hazel's Memoirs: Growing Up in San Francisco." *The Argonaut: The Journal of the San Francisco Museum and Historical Society* 12, no. 2 (Winter 2001).

Skuse, Dick, ed. *Olympic Club of San Francisco: Centennial Yearbook.* 1960.

Sloan, Doris. *Geology of the San Francisco Bay Region.* Berkeley: University of California Press, 2006.

Smallwood, Charles A. *White Front Cars of San Francisco.* South Gate, CA: Interurbans Special 44, 1971.

Sullivan, Deirdre L. *Letting Down the Bars: Race, Space, and Democracy in San Francisco, 1936–1964.* Ph.D. thesis, University of Pennsylvania, 2003.

Sunset City and Sunset Scenes, being views of California Midwinter Fair and Famous Scenes in the Golden State. San Francisco: H. S. Crocker, 1894.

Sunstream Homes: 50 Golden Years of Home Building Excellence (brochure), undated.

Totah, Paul. *Spiritus "Magis": 150 Years of St. Ignatius College Preparatory.* San Francisco: St. Ignatius College Preparatory, 2005.

Turner, Patricia, ed. *1906 Remembered: Firsthand Accounts of the San Francisco Disaster.* San Francisco: Friends of the San Francisco Public Library, 1981.

Tweit, Susan J. Illustrations by James Noel Smith. *Seasons on the Pacific Coast: A Naturalist's Notebook.* San Francisco: Chronicle Books, 1999.

Ungaretti, Lorri. *San Francisco's Sunset District.* Charleston, SC: Arcadia Publishing, 2003.

———. *Then & Now: San Francisco's Sunset District.* Charleston, SC: Arcadia Publishing, 2011.

Vose, Clement E. *Caucasians Only: The Supreme Court, the NAACP, and the Restrictive Covenant Cases.* Berkeley: UC Press, 1959.

Warr, Jesse. Interview with Joseph Foreman Cole. May 8, May 17, May 27, and June 8, 1978 (the Bancroft Library, University of California, Berkeley).

Williams, Mary Ada. *Parkside Pranks and Sunset Stunts.* San Francisco: The North Scale Institute, 1986.

Williams, Mary Ada, with stories by George Stanton. *More Parkside Pranks and Sunset Stunts.* San Francisco: The North Scale Institute, 1990.

Wong, Bernard. *Ethnicity and Entrepreneurship: The New Chinese Immigrants in the SF Bay Area.* Needham Heights, MA: Allyn & Bacon, 1998.

Young, Terence. *Building San Francisco Parks, 1850–1930.* Baltimore: Johns Hopkins University Press, 2004.

Newspapers (various dates)

Black Kitten ("Official Bulletin of the SF Press Club")

Bulletin (also known as *San Francisco Bulletin* and *Daily Evening Bulletin)*

Daily Alta California

Los Angeles Times

New York Times

Parkside Pacific

San Francisco Call (also known as *The Morning Call, San Francisco Bulletin,* and *San Francisco News-Call Bulletin)*

San Francisco Chronicle

San Francisco Examiner

San Francisco Independent

San Francisco Monitor

San Francisco News

San Francisco Pacific News

San Francisco Progress

San Francisco Today

South of Market Journal

Sun-Reporter

Sunset Beacon

Sunset Courier

Sunset Journal

Wall Street Journal

Interviewed by the Author

- Stan Adair, February 7, 2003; August 28, 2010
- Steve Aguado, email messages, 2004
- Marcella Ames, February 16, 2003
- Rita Schiller Aldrich, November 26, 2004; October 23, 2008; various dates in February and March 2009
- Jim Ansbro, November 26, 2004; October 23, 2008; February and March 2009
- Chuck Barnhouse, 2003
- Sandy (Neumann) Baumgarten, February 2011
- Mary Lou Schiller Blackfield, November 26, 2004; October 23, 2008; and various dates in February and March 2009
- Larry Boysen, February 2, 2009
- Anita Brew, February 13, 2011
- Peter Brusati, October 17, 2004

- Dorothy Bryant, various dates, 2011
- Andrew Casper, November 6, 2004
- Claudine and Michael Cohen, October 23, 2008
- Wayne Colyer, February 12, 2011
- Steve Cottrell, email message, February 2012
- Michael Doelger, February 9, 2004
- Donna Lou Tritt Schuh Dunn, May 20, 2007
- Jerry Fristo, Sigmund Stern Grove Historical Tour, July 25, 2002
- Ron Galli and Ray Galli Jr., March 5, 2005
- Jack Goldsworthy, October 21, 2007
- Joe and Teresa Hurley, March 26, 2008
- John Keenan, email message, 2011
- Ellen Kieser, July 16, 2003
- Kathy Klingenberg, email messages, 2011
- Frances (Kniffin) Larkin, May 29, 2004
- Leon Levy, March 11, 2002
- Sue (McDonald) Lundblade, email messages, 2011
- Marie McCormack, January 1, 2003
- Thomas McCormack, March 2, 2003
- William McCormack, March 2, 2003
- Valerie (Phillips) Meehan, July 2002
- Charlie Meyers, January 17, 2009
- Woody and Mamie Moy, April 1, 2007
- Catherine (Faulkner) Murphy, January 5, 2008
- Edythe Newman, July 5, 2004
- Frank and Judy O'Brien, December 29, 2009
- Tom O'Toole, email messages, 2011
- Arthur Pira, February 10, 2010
- JoAnne Quinn, email messages, 2010–2011
- Valerie Schmalz, July 2002
- Alex Spotorno, June 26, 2004
- Maureen (McCormack) Sullivan, March 2, 2003
- Fred Van Dyke, June 22, 2002
- Dr. Hugh Visser, May 29, 2004
- Rosemarie Rousseau Wagner, February 12, 2004
- Jeanne (Von Husen) Warden, April 28, 2007
- John Wentzel, January 12, 2008

PHOTO CREDITS

INDEX

DO YOU HAVE STORIES TO SHARE
ABOUT THE SUNSET?

DO YOU HAVE SOMETHING TO ADD
(OR CORRECT) ABOUT THE HISTORY
IN THIS BOOK?

CONTACT THE AUTHOR AND
SHARE YOUR KNOWLEDGE.
YOUR COMMENTS MAY BE ADDED TO THE
WEBSITE WWW.BALANGEROBOOKS.COM

Send an email to info@balangerobooks.com

or

Mail in your comments to
Lorri Ungaretti c/o
Balangero Books
P. O. Box 640076
San Francisco, CA 94164